Ray of Hope

Asha Deep's Journey Towards Inclusion

Deep Kumar & Madhu Singh

BlueRose ONE.com
Stories Matter
NewDelhi • London

BLUEROSE PUBLISHERS
India | U.K.

BlueRose ONE.com
Stories Matter
NewDelhi • London

For permissions requests or inquiries regarding this publication, please contact:

BLUEROSE PUBLISHERS
www.BlueRoseONE.com
info@bluerosepublishers.com
+91 8882 898 898
+4407342408967

ISBN: 978-93-5741-670-2

Cover design: Tahira
Typesetting: Tanya Raj Upadhyay

First Edition: June 2024

ACKNOWLEDGEMENT

I express my deep indebtedness and gratitude to **Almighty God,** the eternal source of all knowledge and wisdom, for the inspiration, showers of blessings, and strength I received for the successful completion of this thesis.

I express my sincere gratitude to my well-experienced and committed guide, **Prof. (Dr.) Madhu Singh,** for her valuable supervision, availability, and unconditional accompaniment throughout my research. This work would have remained only a distant dream without her professional touch and supervision.

My God-given mother, **Sr. Philo D'Couto,** has been a special person in my life, helping me reach this stage. I am also grateful and proud to all the members of the **Institute of the Maids of the Poor, Barabanki**, for their love, care, motivation, prayers, unconditional support, and blessings. My sincere thanks to **Mala Sinha** and **Abhishek** for their unconditional support. I am deeply grateful to **Pankaj Karan** for his unwavering support and encouragement in completing this demanding and diligent project.

I am grateful to all the professors and non-teaching staff of **St. Xavier's College of Education (Autonomous), Patna,** for their constructive suggestions and encouragement to complete my work.

My sincere thanks to **Sr. Pushpita Chathamalil, Provincial Superior, SCSC, Sr. Lissil Pallipadan, SCSC, Principal**, teaching faculty, support staff, parents, and the students of Asha Deep Rehabilitation Center for Divyangjan, Patna, who helped me wholeheartedly in the course of data collection.

I am thankful to all my friends and well-wishers for their unconditional support during my research work.

Dr. Deep Kumar
Assistant Professor
St. Xavier's College of Education (Autonomous)
Affiliated to Aryabhatta Knowledge University
Patna, Bihar,

ABBREVIATIONS AND ACRONYMS

CRPD	Convention on the Rights of Persons with Disabilities
DEPWP	Department of Empowerment of Persons with Disabilities
GIF	Global Indicator Framework
IAEG-SDGs	Inter-Agency and Expert Group on SDG Indicators
ICF	International Classification of Functioning, Disability and Health
ISO	International Organization for Standardization
IYDP	International Year of Disabled Persons
MoSJE	Ministry of Social Justice & Empowerment
NGO	Non-governmental organization
NIF	National Indicator Framework
NSO	National Statistical Office
NSS	National Sample Survey
NSSO	National Sample Survey Office
PMKVY	Pradhan Mantri Kaushal Vikas Yojana
PwD	Persons with Disabilities

RCI	Rehabilitation Council of India
RPWD	Rights of Persons with Disabilities
SC	Scheduled Caste
SDG	Sustainable Development Goals
SEND	Special Educational Needs and Disabilities
ST	Scheduled Tribe
UN WPA	United Nation World Peace Association
UNESCAP	United Nations Economic and Social Commission for Asia and the Pacific
UNICEF	United Nations Children's Fund
UNSC	United Nations Security Council
UT	Union Territory
WG	Washington Group
WHO	World Health Organisation

TABLE OF CONTENTS

Chapter 1
Introduction

- Introduction
- Historical Background of Asha Deep Rehabilitation Center for Divyangjan
- Mission and Vision of Asha Deep Rehabilitation Center for Divyangjan
- Aims And Objectives of Asha Deep Rehabilitation Centre for Divyangjan
- Creating an Inclusive Society for Divyangjan

Introduction

In the earliest early cultures, particularly in Egypt, Greece, and Rome, disabled new-borns were killed because they were believed to be defective. The guiding principle was that nothing should be presented that was not perfect. During the middle Ages, when profound religious beliefs spread throughout the world, some humanitarian care for children with exceptional needs was provided. The chances of survival for infants with special needs increased, but they were still perceived as being cursed, under the wrath of God, or suffering from divine vengeance for sin. However, throughout history, there have been individuals who have viewed infirmity as a disease. Many people barely hardly even knew they existed.

The Indian government has put a lot of effort into offering a wide range of services for the education of children with disabilities over the past 50 years. The Integrated Education for Disabled Students (IEDC) initiative was started in 1974 to give students with impairments, equal chances in regular schools and help them stay in school. The National Educational Policy (1986), aimed to "integrate the handicapped with the general community at all levels as equal partners, preparing them for normal growth, and enabling them to face life with courage and confidence". The 1990 adoption of the World Declaration on 'Education for All' (EFL) gave the nation's various processes a boost.

A professional training programme was formed by the Rehabilitation Council of India Act of 1992 to meet the needs of students with disabilities. Aiming to clarify the parameters within which the government, public sector, and private sector must act to ensure a dignified existence for disabled persons and aid for their caregivers, the National Policy for Persons with Disabilities was issued in 2006. Right of Children to Free and Compulsory Education (2009), guarantees free and compulsory education to all children between the ages of six and fourteen. According to Chapter V of the PwD Act, every child with a disability has the right to a free education up until the age of eighteen. To achieve the Education for All (EFA) goal by 2010, the Indian government accelerated the new Inclusive Education programme. The goal of inclusion is to include a variety of learners, including those who have impairments, speak other languages and cultures, come from various homes and families, and have diverse interests and learning styles. Regardless of their abilities or weaknesses, all students are included in mainstream education under the umbrella of inclusive education. India's education policy is placing more of an emphasis on kids and persons with special needs, with inclusive education in regular schools being a major governmental objective.

One way in which inclusive education can be achieved is through special schools. Special schools are educational establishments that serve the needs of students with disabilities or unique educational needs. These schools provide specialized instruction, support, and services to help students reach their full potential. In addition to academic instruction, special schools may offer therapies such as speech and language therapy, occupational therapy, and physical therapy, as well as assistive technology and other accommodations to meet the individual needs of students.

Moreover, special schools can also serve as a model for inclusive practices. Special schools can demonstrate the value of inclusion and encourage other educational institutions to follow similar methods by offering a friendly and inclusive atmosphere for students with special needs. This is one way that special schools can support the development of an inclusive culture throughout the entire educational system.

1.1 Importance of Education

Education, in its true sense, promotes a person's growth and independence, enabling him or her to vastly increase in love and compassion. That is what we should be worried about, rather than trying to mould the child into some idealised image. Education's most essential purpose is to build a well-rounded individual capable of dealing with all areas of life.

Every person's life is influenced by their education. It aids in the development of character, views, and intelligence. Education is a tool for bettering one's life. It is, without doubt, the most crucial instrument for transforming one's life. A child's education starts at home. It is a process that lasts a lifetime. Education has a significant impact on the quality of a person's life. Education enhances one's knowledge, talents, and personality as well as attitude. Most importantly, education has an impact on people's career prospects. A well-educated person has a better chance of landing a decent career.

The first stage in education is to learn to read and write. Most information is conveyed via writing. As a result, a lack of writing ability implies losing out on a lot of data. As a result, education helps individuals become literate. Many impoverished individuals seem to better their lives as a result of education. Education also has a role in improving communication. A person's speech is improved and refined. Individuals also enhance various forms of communication as a result of education.

Education improves a person's ability to utilise technology. Education does, without a doubt, teach the technical abilities required for utilising technology. As a result, without education, it would be impossible to operate sophisticated machinery. Education aids in the maturation of individuals. Sophistication infiltrates the lives of educated individuals. Above all, education instils in people the virtue of self-discipline. Educated individuals are also more aware of the value of time. Time is comparable to money to educated individuals. Finally, education allows people to effectively convey their opinions. Individuals with a higher level of education are better able to articulate their viewpoints. As a result, educated individuals are more likely to persuade others of their point of view.

Education allows everyone to have a positive outlook on the world and society and aids in the acquisition of new ideas and the exploration of new concepts. Every community relies heavily on education. It provides a sense of purpose, social position, global knowledge, and the ability to travel. The following are the other benefits of being educated:

i Increase Longevity

To achieve a good job and preserve financial security in life, education is needed. This might imply that one has specialised expertise in a specific field or that one is knowledgeable about a wide range of topics. Education is essential to learn, developing, and thriving in the real world.

ii Instil Values

Education allows us to learn about various values and morals in order to maintain a well-balanced and open mind.

iii Build Self-Assurance

A child who learns to read and write develops confidence in both their abilities and in themselves. It remains the same as the child gets older as time passes. Feeling good about who you are and what you know helps you feel more confident.

iv Creates Possibilities

If the child has an excellent education, he is more likely to have more opportunities in life.

v Encourages Critical Thinking

Children gain critical thinking abilities in a new manner as a result of education, and these talents will continue with them long after they graduate.

vi Builds Communication Skills

Children and adults are taught how to collaborate with others as part of their education. Education teaches interpersonal skills to students, whether they are peers or of a range of different ages. Some of these abilities include how to interact with people in society, how to have a discussion with others, and how to collaborate on various activities.

vii Helps to Develop Character

Learning about diverse cultures, languages, and how other people think and live helps to develop character.

viii Provide for Basic Needs

If anyone has a decent education, he can fulfill basic needs in life. He learns other useful life skills as well as how to dress and take care of himself Education can help get employment and housing when becoming older.

ix Develops Expertise

Education may educate youngsters with more than just book smart; it can also teach knowledge in areas such as art, history, and music. When it comes to education, the sky is the limit. One can enrolin courses if one wants to live a life full of learning chances. It makes no difference whether the person is young or elderly.

1.2 The Concept of Inclusive Education

UNESCO defines inclusion as "a process of recognizing and reacting to the variety of needs of all learners via expanding involvement in learning, cultures, and communities, and eliminating exclusion within and from education, it entails adjustments and revisions in content, techniques, structures, and tactics, with a shared vision that encompasses all children of the proper age range and a belief that it is the regular system's obligation to educate all children."

UNESCO views inclusion as a dynamic approach to responding positively to human diversity and seeing individual differences focusing not as a problem, but as an opportunity that helps in enriching learning. Therefore, a move towards inclusion is not just a simple technical or organizational change but also a movement with a clear philosophy. To implement inclusion effectively, countries need to define their way of inclusive principles together with practical ideas that will guide the transition toward policies that are addressing inclusion in education. Various international declarations that are set in the background of following the principles are always used as a foundation. Every country can use these declarations according to their circumstances depending on their adaptation context.

The idea of inclusive education was established at the **"World Conference on Special Needs Education: Access and Quality"** known as the **Salamanca Statement**, Spain, 1994 (UNESCO, 1994) and was reaffirmed at the World Education Forum in 2000. (Dakar, Senegal 2000). The Statement calls on governments to make ensure that education systems are inclusive and given a top priority and to make the idea of inclusive education a national goal. The United Nations Standard Rules on Equalization of Opportunities for Persons with Disabilities Proclaiming 'Participation and Equality for All' further supports the concept of inclusion. Inclusive Education (IE) is described as a process of removing obstacles to and within the learning environment in order to meet the unique needs of all learners. It entails enrolling in the child's local school's age-appropriate class and receiving specially tailored help (UNICEF 2007). Inclusive education is a method of improving the educational system's ability to reach out to all students. The goals for 'Education for All' were defined during the Jomtien World Conference in Thailand in 1990, and it was declared that every individual (child, youth, and adult) should be able to benefit from educational opportunities that satisfy their fundamental learning requirements. Inclusion is a concept and educational strategy that gives all pupils more opportunities for academic and social success. This covers a wide range of social, recreational, arts, sports, music, day-care and after-school care, extracurricular, faith-based, and other activities.

In India, the National Council of Educational Research and Training (NCERT) teamed up with UNICEF to create 'Project Integrated Education for Disabled Children' (PIED) in 1987, with the goal of improving the integration of disabled students into regular classrooms. The notion of inclusive education has been expanded to include all children who may be disadvantaged, not only those with disabilities. The National Curriculum Framework (NCF-2005), which reaffirms the importance of including and retaining all children in school through a programme that reaffirms the value of each child and enables all children to experience dignity and the confidence to learn, was developed as a result of this broader understanding of the curriculum.

On the one hand, inclusive education is a human rights problem, and on the other, it is a method for transforming a kid into a healthy personality capable of not only living in a society but also competing with others without fear of failure or a complex. Inclusion in school not only develops but also promotes moral principles such as equality, equal opportunity, human rights, and a healthy and happy mindset. It leads to liberation from preconceptions and biases, whether racial or socioeconomic, which breed enmity among individuals who share a society.

Only after understanding the theory underlying Inclusive Education can the notion be operationalized. It is well understood that a hesitant society would be unable to give equal rights to all its students. Inclusion necessitates a paradigm shift in thought. The strategic intervention includes inclusive education. Inclusive education aims to meet the needs of all students while simultaneously resisting discriminatory forces. Inclusion is providing a youngster with a handicap with a comparable environment and experiences as his or her non-disabled classmates. Greater knowledge of the inclusion philosophy would help us achieve clarity on the topic and make certification of inclusion procedures easier.

In order to react to the variety of learners, inclusion necessitates a reorganization of school cultures, policies, and practices. When several common understandings of Inclusive Education are investigated, it can be inferred that many definitions refer to an Inclusive School as one that educates "all" students.

Inclusion does not only mean allowing previously excluded students to return to regular classrooms. It is not about shutting down an ineffective segregated system and putting these students into an unmodified mainstream system. Existing school systems will have to alter in terms of physical characteristics, curricular components, teaching standards and approaches, and leadership responsibilities. This is because Inclusive Education is about all children and young people participating in school and eliminating all sorts of discriminatory behaviours.

Inclusion is a concept that may be characterised as an attitude or a commitment to value diversity and recognise that all students can be taught to their full potential in a common school. It necessitates boosting the ability of traditional institutions to adapt creatively to growing diversity. It also entails developing instructors' abilities to cope with a varied student population and acquiring pedagogical qualities that aid students' learning in the classroom.

Inclusive Education is championed as a tool to reduce obstacles, increase results, and eradicate discrimination. On the other hand, is a complicated and controversial notion with numerous and varied expressions. Inclusion entails offering appropriate solutions to a wide range of learning demands in both official and informal educational settings. Rather than being a side issue about how certain students may be absorbed into mainstream education, inclusive education is a strategy for transforming educational institutions and other learning settings to accommodate the variety of students. Its goal is to help instructors and students feel at ease with variety and perceive it as a challenge and enrichment to the learning environment rather than a hindrance. Inclusion stresses giving opportunity for those with impairments (physical, social, and/or emotional) to participate equally in general education wherever feasible while leaving open the possibility of personal choice and special support and facilities for those who need them.

The term "inclusion" refers to the process of identifying and removing obstacles. As a result, it entails gathering, integrating, and assessing data from a range of sources in order to prepare for policy and practice changes. It is all about leveraging multiple types of evidence to encourage creativity and problem-solving. All pupils must be present, participate, and accomplish in order to be considered included. Here, "presence" refers to where children are educated, as well as how consistently and punctually they attend those institutions; "participation" refers to the quality of their experiences while they are there, and thus must include the learners' perspectives; and "achievement" refers to the outcomes of learning across the curriculum, rather than just test or examination results.

Inclusion places a special focus on groups of students who are in danger of marginalisation, exclusion, or underachievement. This implies a moral obligation to guarantee that those groups classified as statistically "at risk" are closely watched and, when required, efforts made to secure their presence, engagement, and accomplishment in the educational system. As put, it in their proposal for an Index for Inclusion, "inclusion is about creating schools helpful and engaging environments for both staff and students." It's about creating communities that support and celebrate their accomplishments."

1.3 Understanding Disability

A disability is defined as a condition or function that is severely impaired in comparison to an individual's or group's customary standard. Physical disability, sensory impairment, cognitive impairment, intellectual impairment, mental illness, and many forms of chronic disease are all examples of individual functioning.

The ICF (International Categorization of Functioning, Disability, and Health) recognises three aspects of disability:

(i) Structure and function of the human body (and impairment thereof)

(ii) Involvement (and activity restrictions)

(iii) Participation required (and participation restrictions)

Disability is seen as a multifaceted experience for the individual who is affected. Organs or body parts may be affected, as well as a person's involvement in other aspects of life.

1.4 Historical Perspective of Models of Disability

The changing attitudes about disability have resulted in a wide range of legislation and behaviours. The different models of disability put varying duties on states in terms of actions to be performed, and they reflect substantial shifts in how disability is seen. The four basic recognized formulations of disability are the charity model, the bio-centric model, the functional model, and the human rights model.

The Charity Model

The charity mode resulted in a custodial care paradigm, which isolated and marginalized people with disabilities. Regrettably, the model's influence may still be recognized in certain present activities. The findings of an investigation conducted by India's National Human Rights Commission between 1997 and 1999, confirmed that many mental health institutions continue to be managed and administered using the custodial model of care, which is prison-like. These institutions served as incarceration centers for persons with mental diseases, due to catastrophes like the one at "Erwadi" in Tamil Nadu when more than 27 detainees died.

The Bio-centric Model

Disability is seen as a medical or hereditary disease in today's bio-centric understanding of disability. The suggestion is that handicapped people and their families should try to achieve "normalcy" via medical treatments and miracles. As stated in the Position Paper of National Focus Group on Education of Children with Special Needs, Tomlinson (1982) said that charity and bio-centric models arose from the "vested interests" of professionals and the elite to keep the disabled "uneducable" or declare them mentally retarded children and keep them out of the mainstream school system, with special schools serving as a "safety valve" for mainstream schools. (NCERT, 2006)

The Functional Model

In the functional model, a person's right to exercise his or her rights is distinguished based on assessments of individual incapacity and the degree to which a person is seen to be self-sufficient in exercising his or her rights. For example, a child's right to education is contingent on his or her ability to attend school and participate in the classroom, rather than on the school system's ability to accommodate children with impairments.

The Human Rights Model

The human rights model recognizes disability as a significant aspect of human civilization and asserts that all people are born with certain inherent rights and the government should help them not only by enhancing their access to public freedom but also should see that their rights are not hampered by others.

1.5 Types of Disabilities listed under the Rights of Persons with Disabilities (RPWD) Act 2016

Different types of deficiencies have been recognized by the government of India in order to provide special benefits to those in real need. A list of 21 deficiencies identified by the Government of India is listed under the Rights of Persons with Disabilities (RPWD) Act 2016.

(i) Visually Impaired
Visual impairment is defined as the state of not being able to see and not being able to see. Visually impaired people may differ in different limits different individuals. In a strict sense, the term vision impairment refers to the state of total blackness of vision, the inability to distinguish darkness from bright light in both eyes of a person.

(ii) Low-Vision
Low vision is related to a situation where a person has any of the following conditions namely: Visual light not

exceeding 6/18 or less than 20/60 to 3/60 or up to 10/200 (Snellen) in the eye for better resolution with the best resolution; or Vision field limit that removes an angle of fewer than 40 degrees to 10 degrees.

(iii) Leprosy-Cured Persons

Leprosy, also known as Hansen's disease (HD), is a chronic infection caused by the bacterium Mycobacterium leprosy. The disease mainly affects the skin, peripheral nerves, mucous surfaces of the upper respiratory tract, and eyes. Leprosy is known to affect people of all ages, from early childhood to incredible old age.

(iv) Hearing Impairment

Hearing loss occurs when there is a problem or damage to one or more areas of the ear. Transient hearing loss is caused by a problem with the outer or middle ear, including the ear canal, or ossicles. Hearing impairment is the inability to hear in part or in whole. It is a disability, which is divided into two categories, deaf and hard of hearing.

"Deaf" is the frequency of speech in both ears at 70 Decibels.

"Hard to hear" refers to hearing loss in both ears at speed of 60 to 70 Decibels.

(v) Locomotor Disability

Locomotor disability is a problem in moving from one place to another, i.e., disability in the legs. But, in general, it is taken to be related to the inability to relate to bones, joints, and muscles. It causes problems in a person's movements (such as walking, lifting, or holding hands).

(vi) Dwarfism

Dwarfism is a condition that develops as a result of a genetic or medical condition. Dwarfism is usually defined as the height of an adult is 4 feet 10 inches (147 cm) or less. The average age for dwarfism is 4 feet (122 cm). Many different medical conditions cause dwarfism. Dwarfism is seen as a growth disorder characterized by shorter than average body height.

(vii) Intellectual Disability

Also known as Cognitive disability, is a condition characterized by a significant range of cognitive functioning (rational, learning, problem-solving) and adaptive functioning in daily life activities like communication and living independently.

(viii) Mental Illness

Mental illness or mental disorder refers to a significant disorder of thought, mood, perception, orientation, or memory that severely affects the ability to judge, behave, recognize reality, or meet the normal demands of life. But it is also a state of a person's arrested or incomplete state of mind, which is characterized by the subconscious nature of intelligence.

(ix) Autism Spectrum Disorder

Autism Spectrum Disorder (ASD) is a neurological and developmental disorder that affects communication and behaviour. Autism can be diagnosed at any age. But still, it is called a "developmental disorder" because symptoms usually appear in the first two years of life. Autism affects the overall cognitive, emotional, social, and physical health of the person affected.

x) Cerebral Palsy

Cerebral palsy (CB) is a disabling physical condition in which muscle coordination is impaired due to damage to the brain. It occurs during or before childbirth. Cerebral palsy is not a progressive condition, which means it will not get worse over time. Currently, there is no cure for this condition.

(x) Muscular Dystrophy

Muscular dystrophy is a group of inherited diseases that damage and makes the body weaken even if it puts affects the muscles over time. This damage and weakness are caused by a deficiency of the protein dystrophin, which is essential for normal muscle function. Lack of this protein can cause problems with walking, swallowing, and muscle coordination and it gets worse over time.

(xi) Chronic Neurological Conditions

Chronic Neurological Diseases - Alzheimer's disease, Parkinson's disease, dystonia, ALS (Lou Kehric disease), Huntington's disease, neuromuscular disease, multiple sclerosis, and epilepsy, affect millions worldwide and cause the greatest morbidity and mortality.

Examples of Chronic Neurological Conditions:

a Alzheimer's disease and Dementia

b Parkinson's disease

c Dystonia

d ALS (Lou Gehrig's disease)

e Huntington's disease

f neuromuscular disease

g Multiple sclerosis

h Epilepsy

i Stroke

(xii) Specific Learning Disabilities

Specific learning disabilities are a group of disabling conditions that cause a person's ability to hear, think, speak, write, pronounce, or do mathematical calculations. One or more of these abilities may be impaired. A specific learning disorder is a neurodevelopmental disorder that begins at school age but is not recognized until adulthood.

(xiii) Multiple Sclerosis

In multiple sclerosis (MS), the body's immune system attacks the central nervous system, which includes the brain and spinal cord. As a result of MS, the envelope of mail containing neurons is damaged. It exposes the nerve fibers and causes problems with the flow of information through the veins. Over time, MS can lead to permanent damage to the nerves. People with MS experience a variety of symptoms. Due to the nature of the disease, the symptoms vary from person to person. Two of the most common symptoms are fatigue and difficulty walking.

(xiv) Speech and Language Disability

Permanent disability arising from conditions such as laryngitis or aphasia affecting one or more components of speech and language for organic or neurological reasons.

(xv) Thalassemia

Thalassemia is a genetic disorder characterized by low or abnormal hemoglobin production. As we know, hemoglobin is a protein found in red blood cells and is responsible for carrying oxygen in the body. Thalassemia is caused by the destruction of many red blood cells, leading to anaemia. As a result of anemia, a person with thalassemia will have pale skin, fatigue, and dark colour urine.

(xvi) Hemophilia

Hemophilia is often a hereditary genetic disorder that reduces the body's ability to form blood clots, a process that is necessary to stop bleeding. This causes people to bleed for a long time after the risk of injury, easy abrasion, and increased bleeding into the joints or brain. The disease is characterized by a deficiency of blood clotting proteins. In the absence of these proteins, bleeding may last longer than normal. Haemophilia always occurs in men, and they get it from their mothers. Women rarely suffer from hemophilia.

(xvii) Sickle Cell Disease

Sickle cell disease is a group of blood disorders that cause red blood cells (RBCs) to rupture, misalign, and break down. The oxygen-carrying capacity of such misshapen RBCs is significantly reduced. It is a genetically modified disease. A sickle cell disease is a group of disorders that affect hemoglobin, the molecule in red blood cells that provides oxygen to cells throughout the body. People with this disease have strange hemoglobin molecules called hemoglobin S, which can disrupt red blood cells in the form of scythes or crescents.

(xviii) Multiple Disabilities Including Hearing Impaired

Multiple disabilities are simultaneous occurrences of two or more disabling conditions that affect learning or other important life functions. These disorders may be a combination of both motor and emotional nature. Deaf (visual impairment + hearing impairment) visual impairment + hearing impairment + mental impairment.

Visual impairment + mental retardation. Cerebral palsy + mental retardation/hearing/speech / visual problems.

(xix) Acid Attack

An acid attack victim is a person who has been disfigured by violent attacks by throwing acid or a similarly corrosive substance. An acid attack involves a pre-emptive blow to a victim, usually in the face. In addition to causing psychological trauma, acid attacks can cause severe pain, permanent degeneration, subsequent infections, and often blindness in one or both eyes.

(xx) Parkinson's Disease

Parkinson's disease is a brain disorder that leads to difficulty in shaking, erection and walking, balance, and coordination. Symptoms of Parkinson's usually begin gradually and worsen over time. As the disease progresses, people may have difficulty walking and talking. Parkinson's disease (PD) is a central nervous system disorder that affects movement. Parkinson's disease is characterized by tremors and stiffness. It is a progressive disease, which worsens over time. No treatment is currently available.

1.6 Equal Opportunities for All: The Drive Towards Inclusion

When looking at a wide variety of individual needs, education confronts a wide range of cultural and social backgrounds of community-forming groups. Sometimes cultural and social backgrounds can have a negative impact and lead to social exclusion and social exclusion from meaningful contributions to the lives of their communities. Such exclusion, in turn, reduces the opportunities for people to learn, grow and develop. A human rights approach to disability issues has significant implications for the provision of education. Educational limits tend to categorize students with disabilities as defined by alternative limits. Students with disabilities are usually placed in special schools or classes or are completely excluded from any educational opportunity on the grounds that they are 'severely disabled. This usually results in Literacy and low skills, especially among adults with disabilities, contributing to high levels of unemployment and poverty. However, democratic society has developed an opinion that all educated people, regardless of the education level, are nothing but quality education and training Lifelong learning, meaningful participation in the community as a working world, and productive citizens. So, anything the education and training system must play an important role in improving the quality of life and facing developmental challenges for all people. "Education must take on the difficult task of transforming diversity into a constructive contributing to mutual understanding between individuals and groups" (UNESCO).

The adjusted education system that facilitates modern-level knowledge and skills is one of the most important components of positive change and the successful development of a community. The use of technology is not the only requirement of the new century. There is also a greater emphasis on academic planning and policy classification. Any education policy can face different challenges, and each can find his / her place in the community to which they belong, while at the same time paving the way for opening in other communities.

It has been recognized that current strategies and programs are often inadequate or inappropriate to meet the needs of children, adolescents, and adults affected by marginalization and exclusion. Currently, international education and social policy tend to target those at risk of exclusion, integrate them into society and provide them with access and quality basic education. In essence, this approach is based on the philosophy of social integration, which considers the diversity of strengths, abilities, and needs to be natural and desirable, bringing the opportunity for any community to respond to the community in ways that lead to learning and development., Giving each member a valuable role.

Historically, the term 'enrolment' often refers to moving disabled children to major institutions or reducing the exclusion of other students from school. It has now been acknowledged the inclusion of children with disabilities requires not only their integration but also changes in the current policies, practices, and attitudes of the community without providing them with the support they need. In the first case, the enrolment movement is extended to the category of persons who have lost the opportunity to receive an education, thereby gaining a full share in the life of the community, congenital or acquired disabilities, socio-economic loss, war conflicts or other negative factors - barriers to learning.

1.7 Creating an Inclusive Society for Persons with Disabilities

Making adaptations for people with disabilities is essential to ensure that everyone is appreciated, respected, and given an equal opportunity to take part in society. Sadly, obstacles prevent persons with disabilities from fully participating in a variety of everyday activities, including education, job, transportation, and social interactions. But there are many ways that people and organisations may work to make the world more accepting of those with disabilities. Some of the ways could be:

(i) To educate ourselves and others about their needs and experiences:

Education about the needs and experiences of those with disabilities is one of the most crucial steps we can take to ensure their inclusion. This can entail gaining knowledge about the many sorts of disabilities, comprehending the difficulties that those with disabilities encounter, and being aware of the tools and resources that can be used to assist them. By broadening our knowledge and comprehension, we can support those with disabilities more effectively and seek to remove obstacles that keep them from participating fully in society.

(ii) Accessibility:

Another key aspect of creating inclusion for people with disabilities is to ensure that physical spaces and environments are accessible to everyone. This can involve making modifications to buildings, transportation systems, and public spaces to ensure that they are accessible to people with mobility impairments, visual impairments, hearing impairments, and other disabilities. For example, installing wheelchair ramps, elevators, and accessible restrooms can make a huge difference in enabling people with mobility impairments to navigate public spaces.

(iii) Employment:

Another area where it is critical to include people with disabilities is the workplace. Many people with disabilities encounter difficulties in obtaining and retaining employment, which can result in financial instability and exclusion from the workforce. Nonetheless, companies can foster a more inclusive workplace that persons with disabilities can achieve by providing reasonable adjustments, such as flexible hours or assistive technology. In order to boost the presence of individuals with disabilities in the workforce, employers should actively seek out candidates with disabilities and ensure that job ads are accessible.

(iv) Social Inclusion:

It is crucial to include people with disabilities in social and leisure activities. Due to physical or other obstacles, people with disabilities are frequently excluded from social gatherings and activities. Yet, we can make a more welcoming and inclusive environment for everyone by actively working to include persons with disabilities in social events, such as by offering sign language interpreters or other accommodations.

(v) Financial Inclusion:

The provision of inexpensive financial products and services to the underprivileged sector of society is known as financial inclusion. This comprises financial services including insurance, retirement plans, and loans for a range of uses as well as banking goods.

(vi) Use of Assistive Technology (AT) :

An assistive technology is any adaptive device or service that helps a student with a disability's participation, performance, or independence. With the aid of assistive technology, visually impaired people—both those with and without additional disabilities—can access more of the prescribed curriculum and perform better academically.

In conclusion, promoting inclusion for those with disabilities is essential to guarantee that everyone is valued, respected, and given an equal chance to participate in society. We may work to remove obstacles and create a more inclusive society for all by educating ourselves and others, making sure physical venues are accessible, advocating inclusive employment practices, and actively integrating people with disabilities in social events.

1.8 Inclusive Education and Constitutional Role

Inclusive Education can benefit those children directly who have learning disabilities, mild or borderline intellectual functioning, and other children with disabilities. There are schools that have adopted a separate way of assessing these children instead of the normal way of assessments. The oral assessment is given priorities, and projects that these children can understand and can do easily are given. Many times, some experimental methods of learning are also used for their training. Activities are designed in such a way that they take care of the co-curricular assessments that prove to be beneficial for these children. Schools even provide special resource rooms with trained resource instructors and adequate learning aids that make it possible for these children to grow in an incredibly positive way. These kinds of facilities should be made compulsory in all schools to make sure they adapt to inclusive education.

As we see the availability of abundant opportunities across different fields, be it, music, sports, martial arts, art, and craft, children with disabilities can excel across multiple myriad fields with basic academics and adequate life skills.

Different TV channels organize different talent shows in which these children take part in different capacities and have touched many hearts present in the shows. Many times, it has been seen that they do much better than any normal child. This gives a clear message to society that if these children are given proper training and platform, there are chances they can excel on their own. This is the right way where the current education system of our country needs to focus on empowering children with disabilities.

There are many Inclusive school communities that have educational settings that provide students with disabilities to have equal opportunities to participate and receive support in different aspects of school life alongside peers who do not have disabilities. In an inclusive system, there are special educators, the need specialized instructional supports personnel, general educators, and other education personnel to work together to take care of the needs of the students with disabilities. This opens the door for collaboration with these educators for better support and learning. This also gives an opportunity for the students to participate and develop their talents. The research demonstrates that a learning community is called to be better, richer, and more effective than helping disabled students to have full participation in learning and development.

The Directive Principle of the Indian Constitution, the National Policy of Education (NPE-1986), The RCI Act, the Persons with Disabilities Act (1996, 2016), and The Sarva Shiksha Abhiyan (SSA 2010), all of them ensure equality for disabled children. They all speak of empowering children to ensure admission, retention, and education of all children in the age group of 6 to 14 years, including the disabled ones. This is an assurance that no normal school can deny admission to any disabled child in any circumstances.

The precedent for inclusive education was set in the Least Restrictive Environment (LRE) clause of Public Law 94-142, originally passed by Congress in the year 1975. The recent version of the law for the disabled is known as the Individuals with Disabilities Education Act (IDEA) which came into force in the year 2004. In the meantime, many strides have been made in realizing the intent of the law, which often helps schools still treat inclusive education. This is a big challenge that supports students with disabilities. We find it very often that separateness and exclusion can be defined in the educational experience, particularly for the students with the most significant cognitive disabilities. The slow rate of implementation and the received challenges involving, different educators, students, and their families it has been found many compelling reasons to support inclusive education for students with and without disabilities.

We see that education is a fundamental human right and it is essential to ensure that all can realize their ability and potential. The main key aim of education is to give all citizens the necessary skills and different values to improve their quality of life and standard of living. These aims can be achieved when we are able to continue to work together to improve access to education and to provide a better quality of educational facilities in an equitable manner.

Inclusion in education involves diversity and recognizes the value of human living. It provides a sense of belonging for every child and their family. It also gives an acceptance of individuality in diversity and different opportunities to all the children who are involved in the curriculum that teaches them and helps them in learning. Every child that attends the school is involved in general education in a classroom day today and is totally involved in learning. These students naturally support and help each other in learning and overcoming the different challenges in the day-to-day life routine. These students are grouped in different groups and are involved in different activities in the classroom which makes the structure more open and flexible. This also gives the group to enhance the individual ability and respect it. Naturally, we also find that the group of students help each other, and they are presumed to be competent. All of them are incredibly supportive of each other in curriculum adaptation and differentiated teaching activities. This group of students is given equal opportunity and so they are known and valued as full members of the school community. They develop meaningful social relationships with their own peers, and they participate in different aspects of their school life. We also find them connected in social media platforms where they act and participate just like any other normal individual.Many apps are made user-friendly and these children with disabilities participate by using them and taking them as active interaction platforms just like any other normal person without a disability.

In the school system Inclusive education adopts a process where strategic plans and policies are adopted. These plans and strategies help to improve and change the teaching strategies for a wider and more diverse range of children who can be taken care of and given proper training. This also helps the families of children with disabilities.

Inclusive education implicitly means identifying the child's needs and learning style and adapting the classroom in such a way that the teaching strategies are to ensure high-quality learning outcomes. These outcomes are helpful for all children in the class.

The United Nations' contribution is very much counted in the field of imparting and caring for the education of disabled children. The United Nations Educational, Scientific and Cultural Organisation (UNESCO) defines inclusive education as a process intended to respond to every student's life. It also speaks of increasing the life of the children and their participation and reducing exclusion within and from education. It gives emphasis on the attendance of the child, their participation in learning, and their achievement. It gives focuses on those children especially those who are excluded due to different reasons, and those who are at risk of being marginalized.

It constitutes an essential element to advance on the EFA agenda. The concept of education for all does not imply the concept of inclusion. Being intended to ensure access to education, inclusion involves access to high-quality education without any discrimination of any kind, within or outside of the school system. This teaching requires an in-depth transformation of the education system that is prevailing in today's day-to-day life. We must accept the concept that without inclusion, certain groups of students are likely to be excluded from the day-to-day activity of social life. Inclusion should be a guiding force and principle that gives direction to our educational policies and programmes so that education can be for all and not only for the majority.

The National Policy of Education (NEP) which was created and came into force in 1986 also gave importance to inclusion in the school system. This was followed by the Integrated Education of Disabled Children (IEDC, 1974) which helped the children to be included in the mainstream of the classrooms. It then spoke of children with 'mild' disabilities should be made part of the mainstream of the classroom, whereas children with 'moderate to severe' disabilities should be placed in segregated special schools mainly that will take care of their needs. The Action Programme of 1992 was also created to implement the guidelines of NPE-1986 stating taking care of special needs children. Broadening the sense and the NPE's definitions of who should be included in the mainstream of schooling and who should not. It defined that the children with a disability to whom it's possible to be educated in the general schools should not be admitted to the special school and they should be part of the normal school system. It also spoke of the children by saying that once children with disabilities acquire basic living skills, which would be learned in resource rooms or special schools, they should be admitted into the mainstream education system.

In the year 1992, we also see the year of the Rehabilitation Council of India (RCI) Act. The RCI Act provides standards for rehabilitation professionals; one type of rehabilitation professional is a special education teacher. In the year 2002, the 86th amendment of the constitution was made that mandated free and compulsory education to all children ages 6-14 and with the help of the World Bank, the Government of India gave a start to Sarva Shiksha Abhiyan – SSA that spoke of Education for all in India.

The Right to Education Act was framed as a 'social justice and collective advocacy perspective' rather than through a framework of individual rights, is not disability-specific, but inclusive of children with disabilities, with specific sections that address the educational rights of students with disabilities. The RTE act was passed in 2009 and put into full effect in 2010.

It was becoming important that our country create a bill around sections 45 and 21 (A) of the constitution that will become the Right to Education Act which was originally floated in 2005. This was the same year when the Ministry of Human Resource Development also drafted the Action Plan for the Inclusion Education of Children and Youth with Disabilities (IECYD). This was an action plan that envisions that all children with special needs will have access to mainstream education. In order to facilitate this plan, the government specifically collaborated between the Rehabilitation Council and the National Council for Teachers Education. It was mainly to ensure that there are adequate numbers of teachers trained to take care of the need of these special children in inclusive education. This was made sure that proper physical and ideological infrastructure facilitated inclusion in schools. This plan specifically took a move from integration towards inclusion stating whereas under the Scheme of Integrated Education of Disabled Children (IEDC) as it stands in the present form. Children with special needs are placed in regular schools without making any changes in the school to accommodate and support diverse needs. The revised IECYD will, in contrast, modify the existing physical infrastructures and teaching methodologies to meet the needs of all children, including children with Special Needs.

The Commission, at its fifty-eighth session, adopted resolution 58/4 of 22nd May 2002 on promoting an inclusive, a barrier-free, and rights-based society for people with disabilities in the Asian and Pacific region in the twenty-first century, by which it proclaimed the extension of the Asian and Pacific Decade of Disabled Persons, 1993-2002, for another decade, 2003-2012 Biwako Millennium Framework (1993-2012).

1.9 Background of the Inclusive Education Programme

The Indian government is constitutionally obliged to ensure that every kid has access to basic education. Since India's independence in 1947, the government has enacted a slew of regulations relating to special education. The Integrated Education for Disabled Children (IEDC) plan of 1974 was one of the first formal efforts made by the Government of India (NCERT, 2011). During the post-independence period, the Kothari Commission (1966) emphasized the significance of teaching children with impairments (Pandey 2006). The Ministry of Welfare of the Government of India recognized the critical need for an organization to oversee and control HRD programmes in the field of disability rehabilitation in the 1980s. 90% of India's estimated 40 million children aged four to sixteen years with physical and mental impairments were excluded from mainstream school until the 1990s. The National Policy on Education (NPE, 1986) and the Programme of Action (1992) both emphasise the need of integrating special needs students with other groups. In 1994–95, the Indian government launched the District Primary Education Project (DPEP).

The idea of inclusive education was incorporated into the District Primary Education Program in the late 1990s (i.e., in 1997). (DPEP). In accordance with global trends, this programme placed a specific emphasis on the integration of children with mild to moderate impairments, and it became one of the GOI's largest flagship programmes at the time, with a budget of 40,000 million rupees (approximately 740 million US dollars). One such programme is the Sarva Shiksha Abhiyan (SSA), which was established in 2001 to accomplish the objective of the Universalization of Elementary Education. Access, enrolment, and retention of all children aged 6 to 14 are three key aspects of UEE. Under the SSA, a zero-rejection policy has been implemented, ensuring that every child with Special Needs (CWSN), regardless of the kind, category, or degree of impairment, receives a relevant and excellent education. The 2005 National Curriculum Framework (NCF) established a clear framework for inclusive education. A National Action Plan for the inclusion of children and teenagers with disabilities in school was adopted by the Ministry of Human Resource Development in 2005. In 2009-10, IEDC was renamed "Inclusive Education of the Handicapped at the Secondary Stage (IEDSS)" to give help for the inclusive education of disabled pupils in respective classes 9th and 10th. Since 2013, this plan has been absorbed into the Rashtriya Madhyamik Shiksha Abhiyan (RMSA). Integration of these youngsters into regular classrooms is critical in order to help them socialize and gain confidence.

1.10 Problems and Challenges of Inclusive Education

The number of children with special needs in India is enormous, their issues are complicated, resources are few, and societal attitudes are harmful. The path to inclusive education is long and winding, with many obstacles and possibilities along the way. India is a multilingual, multicultural, and multireligious country whose people are divided along socioeconomic and caste lines. India is the world's second-most populous country, behind China, with an estimated population of 1,210 million people. It is home to 17% of the world's population and 20% of the world's unschooled youngsters. The goal of inclusion is to provide kids with support. As schools accommodate kids with more diverse origins and skills, the primary goal has grown more difficult. The number of persons with disabilities in India is estimated to be 26 million, or about 2.1 percent of the overall population, according to official figures from the Census of India (Government of India, 2011). However, according to UNICEF's Report on the Status of Disability in India (2000), about 30 million children in India are disabled in some way. Approximately 10% of the world's population has a disability, with 80 percent of these people living in poor nations. However, in India, 75 percent of persons with disabilities reside in rural regions. Since the country's independence, the government has enacted a number of policies concerning special education. In conventional classrooms, there may be several obstacles to educating students with impairments. These difficulties might be caused by a lack of appropriate human and financial resources, unfavourable teacher and community attitudes, and non-disabled classmates and their parents. Despite the Indian government's attempts to develop policies that are inclusive of persons with disabilities, its implementation efforts have not resulted in an inclusive educational system. Furthermore, the number of children dropping out of school is increasing, particularly in low-income communities. Due to their parent's financial difficulties, students are compelled to drop out of school and labour to assist their parents to make ends meet. As a result, the number of child laborers is increasing, resulting in physical and psychological problems. Negative attitudes and behaviour on the part of both instructors and parents with respect to the ability of handicapped children to learn to pose unique problems. Another significant issue is that most handicapped individuals continue to be denied equitable access to mainstream schooling.

In India, large class sizes offer another obstacle to the implementation of inclusive education. In order to teach children with disabilities in inclusive education settings, Das, Kuyini, and Desai (2013) looked at the existing skill levels of normal primary and secondary school instructors in Delhi, India. They discovered that over 70% of normal school instructors had no special education training and had no prior experience teaching kids with impairments. In addition, 87% of instructors lacked access to support services in their classes. According to the Sixth All India Educational Survey (NCERT, 1998), special needs education is required for about 20 million of India's 200 million school-aged children (6–14 years). Even though the national average for gross enrolment in school is above 90%, only about 5% of children with disabilities attend school. For children with impairments, peer acceptance is a much harder problem. Children with disabilities are frequently ridiculed and harassed by their classmates who are not handicapped. A high percentage of disabled children live in households with incomes that are much below the poverty line.

In India, most school employees are unprepared to plan and administer educational programmes for kids with disabilities in normal schools. In India, most teacher education programmes do not include a disability studies course. In India, most schools are poorly constructed, and just a few are prepared to accommodate the special requirements of disabled children. It is also worth mentioning that obtaining and resourcing assistive equipment presents problems.

Despite many attempts in India to promote inclusive education, around 94 percent of children with disabilities were denied access to educational programmes. Over and beyond some of the problems that India has in common with other developing nations, there are certain unique characteristics that will make educational reform extremely difficult to achieve. The Government of India's commitment to the Universalisation of Elementary Education (UEE) would not be completely realised until the special educational needs of physically and mentally challenged children are addressed.

Inclusion is becoming a buzzword in education circles, but there are still a lot of misconceptions about it. We find a lack of confidence in the teachers to teach in inclusive settings. The main reason is that they are mostly not equipped with the latest updated given situation so that they are able to adapt it in their teaching. Many teachers are not trained well to deal with inclusive education. Many teacher training institutions do not support the training in such a manner that the trainees have exposure to the need of special children. Many teachers are not able to handle the methodology that is suited to the educational needs of children with special needs. As we find that the training lacks steps to be taken care of the needy students with special needs the curriculum is not designed in such a way that can cater to their needs. This is a major problem as the curriculum is not according to the time the children are not able to be guided by the teachers helping the children with their needs. Community plays an important role in all this and many times the community itself is not incredibly supportive. So, the problem of mobilizing the community to participate in inclusive education programme is the need of the hour.

An important step taken through legislation is the Right to Persons with special needs Act 2016. This act aimed at reducing the discrimination experienced by the divyangjan. Disability is generally equated with not being able to do something and being incapacity. There is a widespread underestimation of the abilities and potential of divyangjan due to the general public perception that has a prejudiced mind to keep judging. These minds create a vicious cycle of underachievement and think that children with special needs are not able to do anything in life. We very often underestimate the abilities and potential of the divyangjan due to general public perception and prejudices. Many times, we create a vicious cycle of underachievement of our ability. We do not try to understand their capabilities and achievement. The impact of this always keeps them far from life experiences, as we fail to give them opportunities to show their talents and abilities. We always try to keep them in our helping arms and behave as if they need us. We also think they are help seekers even without understanding their feelings. We try to keep them very protective as they always like to stand on their own and do whatever they wish to do. If we guide them in a very proper way and think of their vocational rehabilitation it can be incredibly positive and useful for them. Training in proper time and guidance will make them in person more functional, and psychologically strong, and develop their inner ability. They also develop in their emotional impairments or health disabilities to overcome barriers that help them in their proper growth. As we take care of their vocational rehabilitation the divyangjan totally depends on the psychosocial approach that takes care of every individual in different ways. Every child develops in their individual way in the context of the combined influence that the psychological factors and the surroundings of their social environment have on their physical and mental wellness and growth that helps their ability to function. At times it can be possible that persons may not be fully aware of the relationship between their mental and emotional well-being and the environment. So, everything must be taken care of when we talk about children with special care and special need.

Rights are interconnected and interdependent. In the absence of one, it becomes difficult to enjoy other rights. Despite recognition by the international community of the dignity of human life, Divyangjan have remained marginalized and excluded from participating in different aspects of community life. They have always been perceived as lacking the abilities and potential to engage in any meaningful activity or work. In India, The Right to

Persons with Disabilities Act, of 2016 adopts a multi-prone approach to the issue of employment of Divyangjan.

In order to promote the employment of Divyangjan in the organized formal sector, it provides for a scheme of quota to the extent of 4% in all government departments (Central and State government), public sector undertakings, and local authorities to be distributed equally to the extent of 1% each among persons suffering from blindness and low vision, persons suffering from hearing impairment, and persons suffering from a locomotor disability or cerebral palsy (Section 33)

1.11 From Special Education to Inclusion: How Special School can pave the Way fora More Inclusive Education System

Special schools are educational institutions that cater to the needs of students with special needs or impairments. To enable pupils to realise their best potential, these schools offer specialised instruction, assistance, and services. Special schools may provide therapies including speech and language therapy, occupational therapy, and physical therapy in addition to academic education, as well as assistive technology and other modifications to fit each student's unique needs.

Although the idea of special schools may appear incompatible with that of inclusive education, these institutions can really be quite helpful in fostering inclusion. Special schools can assist students with special needs in overcoming obstacles to learning and succeeding by offering them customised teaching and assistance. When students gain self-assurance and abilities that enable them to take part more completely in academic and social activities, their success can subsequently result in greater inclusion in settings that are more mainstream.

Moreover, special schools can also serve as a model for inclusive practices. Special schools can show the value of inclusion and encourage other educational institutions to follow similar methods by offering a friendly and inclusive atmosphere for kids with special needs. This is one way that special schools can support the development of an inclusive culture throughout the entire educational system.

Ultimately the goal of inclusive education is to provide all students with the opportunity to reach their full potential, and special schools can be an important part of achieving this goal.

Historical Background of Asha Deep Rehabilitation Center for Divyangjan

The Asha Deep Rehabilitation Centre for Divyangjan, Patna was established in the year 1996 by the grace of the sisters of the Holy Cross. It first started with sick children. However, at present, the organization is serving Divyangjancentres across India for thousands of children with disabilities, helping them become effective and useful members of the community. The approach of this system is a very holistic one.

Asha Deep Rehabilitation Centre for Divyangjan aims to improve and activate a person with a disability by developing hearing, speech, and language skills. Children in the school are trained to develop communication skills. Communication skills help them achieve rich and productive lives. Children can communicate through sign language and speak their minds to others. The development of communication skills also helps them to be a part of the mainstream. The school runs on the Bihar Board Curriculum and K.G. Up to Standard X. The inclusive education system is currently a challenge to society, so the gap between a normal school and a special school is being filled by the Asha Deep Rehabilitation Centre for Divyangjan.

The Mercy Sisters of the Holy Cross are eager to bring about a change of attitude in their disabled children, and through their training they seek to make a large-scale change in society. They follow a participatory and integrated approach at all levels. Living in a pluralistic society, they like networking and collaborating with like-minded individuals, groups, and governments. The sisters are moved by the merciful love of the Lord and are inspired by the words of their founders.

"As long as there is a poor child under the sun, I cannot rest."

(Fr. Theodosius Florentini).

"Discover the grain of gold hidden in the heart of every person".

(Mother Maria Theresa Screer)

Aims and Objectives of Asha Deep Rehabilitation Centre for Divyangjan

Asha Deep Rehabilitation Centre for Divyangjan initially aimed to provide joint care through a school livelihood, a hostel, and a vocational training centre for children with intellectual disabilities. The aim is to provide them with all the opportunities for their comprehensive development with the following objectives.

i Education and training for children with intellectual disabilities.

ii Provide vocational training for future employment.

iii To foster mutual assistance between parents to provide advice and assistance through counselling and training.

iv Raising public awareness.

Services provided by Asha Deep Rehabilitation Centre for Divyangjan

For the Hearing Impaired

Early Intervention and Rehabilitation

Pre-School Training

Class I to Class X (Hindi Medium)

Speech Therapy

Matching Hearing Aids

Computer Training

For the Intellectual Disabled

Self-Help Skills and Rehabilitation

Training in Daily Life Skills: Total and optimal motor functions, mealtime activities, dressing, irritability, and labour training.

Preschool Training: Speech and Language, Reading, Writing, Arithmetic

Developing Social and Communication Skills

Sports, Dance, and Vocational Training.

Medical facilities at Asha Deep Rehabilitation Centre for Divyangjan

Speech Therapy

Paediatrician

Psychologist

Play Therapy

Psychiatrist

For the Hearing and Visual Impaired

Asha Deep Rehabilitation Centre for Divyangjan is the only organization that supports hearing-impaired children across Bihar. Education is provided by trained educators to develop daily living skills, communication, and literacy for deaf and blind children. They contribute to the social integration of deaf and blind children by working with families and communities. They support the state-wide network of families of deaf and blind children and meet regularly to share their common concerns and achievements. Through their advocacy effort in Bihar, they are actively pursuing the interest of deaf people.

Asha Deep Rehabilitation Centre for Divyangjan has been successful in enrolling their hearing-impaired students in regular schools under Bihar State Education Board, and their organization has received numerous awards for excellence in academic and co-curricular activities. Many of their children excelled in vocational skills. Many of their students have won awards in sports and painting at the state and national levels. Also, their faculty has received accolades for excellence in teaching and management.

Mission and Vision of Asha Deep Rehabilitation Centre for Divyangjan.

As mentioned in the Brochure of the institution, the following words were said by the founder of the institution.

"Urged by the Lord's compassionate love, challenged by the need of the time, the sisters of Mercy of the Holy Cross are committed to the objectives of upliftment of differently abled children. The sisters strive towards a new society of wholesome individuals, families, and communities where poor and underprivileged children are cared for."

Asha Deep Rehabilitation Centre for the Divyangjan aims at empowering and enabling the person with a disability through developing listening skills, speech skills, and language skills. Children in the rehabilitation centre are trained to develop communication skills. Communication skills enable them to achieve richer and more productive life. Children can communicate through sign language and speak their minds to others. The development of communication skills even helps them to be a part of the mainstream.

Sisters of Mercy of the Holy Cross earnestly desire to bring about an attitudinal change in the disabled children who come to them and through their training, they try to make a change in society at large. They adopt participatory and integrated approaches at all levels. Living in a pluralistic society they want to further their networking and collaboration with like-minded persons, groups, and governments. The sisters of the Holy Cross are moved by the Lord's compassionate Love and are inspired by the words of their founders who had a mission to serve the people in whatever condition they are.

"As long as there is a poor child under the sun, I cannot rest"

(Fr. Theodosius Florentini)

"Discover the grain of gold that is hidden in every person's heart"

(Mother Maria Theresa Scherer)

The Sisters at Asha Deep earnestly desire to bring about attitudinal change in themselves and in society at large.They adopt a participatory and integrated approach at all levels of their involvement. Living in apluralistic society they want to further their networking and collaboration with like-mindedpersons,groups,and government sectors.

Aims And Objectives of Asha Deep Rehabilitation Centre for Divyangjan

Asha Deep Rehabilitation Centre for Divyangjan initially aimed to provide joint care through a school livelihood, a hostel, and a vocational training centre for children with intellectual disabilities. The aim is to provide them with all the opportunities for comprehensive development with the following objectives.

i Education and training for children with intellectual disabilities.

ii Provide vocational training for future employment.

iii To foster mutual assistance between parents to provide advice and assistance through counselling and training.

iv Raising public awareness.

Creating an Inclusive Society for Divyangjan

Making adaptations for people with disabilities is essential to ensure that everyone is appreciated, respected, and given an equal opportunity to take part in society. Sadly, obstacles prevent persons with disabilities from fully participating in a variety of everyday activities, including education, job, transportation, and social interactions. But there are many ways that people and organisations may work to make the world more accepting of those with disabilities. Some of the ways could be:

(i) To educate ourselves and others about their needs and experiences:

Education about the needs and experiences of those with disabilities is one of the most crucial steps we can take to ensure their inclusion. This can entail gaining knowledge about the many sorts of disabilities, comprehending the difficulties that those with disabilities encounter, and being aware of the tools and resources that can be used to assist them. By broadening our knowledge and comprehension, we can support those with disabilities more effectively and seek to remove obstacles that keep them from participating fully in society.

(ii) Accessibility:

Another key aspect of creating inclusion for people with disabilities is to ensure that physical spaces and environments are accessible to everyone. This can involve making modifications to buildings, transportation systems, and public spaces to ensure that they are accessible to people with mobility impairments, visual impairments, hearing impairments, and other disabilities. For example, installing wheelchair ramps, elevators, and accessible restrooms can make a huge difference in enabling people with mobility impairments to navigate public spaces.

(iii) Employment:

Another area where it is critical to include people with disabilities is the workplace. Many people with disabilities encounter difficulties in obtaining and retaining employment, which can result in financial instability and exclusion from the workforce. Nonetheless, companies can foster a more inclusive workplace that persons with disabilities can achieve by providing reasonable adjustments, such as flexible hours or assistive technology. In order to boost the presence of individuals with disabilities in the workforce, employers should actively seek out candidates with disabilities and ensure that job ads are accessible.

(iv) Social Inclusion:

It is crucial to include people with disabilities in social and leisure activities. Due to physical or other obstacles, people with disabilities are frequently excluded from social gatherings and activities. Yet, we can make a more welcoming and inclusive environment for everyone by actively working to include persons with disabilities in social events, such as by offering sign language interpreters or other accommodations.

(v) Financial Inclusion:

The provision of inexpensive financial products and services to the underprivileged sector of society is known as financial inclusion. This comprises financial services including insurance, retirement plans, and loans for a range of uses as well as banking goods.

(vi) Use of Assistive Technology (AT):

An assistive technology is any adaptive device or service that helps a student with a disability's participation, performance, or independence. With the aid of assistive technology, visually impaired people—both those with and without additional disabilities—can access more of the prescribed curriculum and perform better academically.

In conclusion, promoting inclusion for those with disabilities is essential to guarantee that everyone is valued, respected, and given an equal chance to participate in society. We may work to remove obstacles and create a more inclusive society for all by educating ourselves and others, making sure physical venues are accessible, advocating inclusive employment practices, and actively integrating people with disabilities in social events.

Chapter 2
Academic and Non-Academic Activities

Academic and Non-Academic Activities

- Creating an Inclusive Society for Persons with Disabilities
- Programmes organized for Divyangjan
- Programmes organized for Hearing Impaired
- Programmes organized for Divyangjan
- Programmes organized for the Visually Impaired

Introduction

A well-known facility for people with intellectual disability and mental health issues is the Asha Deep Rehabilitation Centre in Patna. The centre provides a wide variety of academic and extracurricular activities geared at enhancing the lives of individuals it serves. Asha Deep, a nonprofit organisation with a focus on empowerment, has emerged as a ray of hope for Patna's disabled population. To meet the particular requirements of its recipients, the organisation has expanded and varied its programmes throughout time.

Creating an Inclusive Society for Persons with Disabilities

Making adaptations for people with disabilities is essential to ensure that everyone is appreciated, respected, and given an equal opportunity to take part in society. Sadly, obstacles prevent persons with disabilities from fully participating in a variety of everyday activities, including education, job, transportation, and social interactions. But there are many ways that people and organisations may work to make the world more accepting of those with disabilities. Some of the ways could be:

(vii) To educate ourselves and others about their needs and experiences:

Education about the needs and experiences of those with disabilities is one of the most crucial steps we can take to ensure their inclusion. This can entail gaining knowledge about the many sorts of disabilities, comprehending the difficulties that those with disabilities encounter, and being aware of the tools and resources that can be used to assist them. By broadening our knowledge and comprehension, we can support those with disabilities more effectively and seek to remove obstacles that keep them from participating fully in society.

(viii) Accessibility:

Another key aspect of creating inclusion for people with disabilities is to ensure that physical spaces and environments are accessible to everyone. This can involve making modifications to buildings, transportation systems, and public spaces to ensure that they are accessible to people with mobility impairments, visual impairments, hearing impairments, and other disabilities. For example, installing wheelchair ramps, elevators, and accessible restrooms can make a huge difference in enabling people with mobility impairments to navigate public spaces.

(ix) Employment:

Another area where it is critical to include people with disabilities is the workplace. Many people with disabilities encounter difficulties in obtaining and retaining employment, which can result in financial instability and exclusion from the workforce. Nonetheless, companies can foster a more inclusive workplace that persons with disabilities can achieve by providing reasonable adjustments, such as flexible hours or assistive technology. In order to boost the presence of individuals with disabilities in the workforce, employers should actively seek out candidates with disabilities and ensure that job ads are accessible.

(x) Social Inclusion:

It is crucial to include people with disabilities in social and leisure activities. Due to physical or other obstacles, people with disabilities are frequently excluded from social gatherings and activities. Yet, we can make a more welcoming and inclusive environment for everyone by actively working to include persons with disabilities in social events, such as by offering sign language interpreters or other accommodations.

(xi) Financial Inclusion:

The provision of inexpensive financial products and services to the underprivileged sector of society is known as financial inclusion. This comprises financial services including insurance, retirement plans, and loans for a range of uses as well as banking goods.

(xii) Use of Assistive Technology (AT) :

An assistive technology is any adaptive device or service that helps a student with a disability's participation, performance, or independence. With the aid of assistive technology, visually impaired people—both those with and without additional disabilities—can access more of the prescribed curriculum and perform better academically.

In conclusion, promoting inclusion for those with disabilities is essential to guarantee that everyone is valued, respected, and given an equal chance to participate in society. We may work to remove obstacles and create a more inclusive society for all by educating ourselves and others, making sure physical venues are accessible, advocating inclusive employment practices, and actively integrating people with disabilities in social events.

- **Academic pursuits include:**

1. Daily living activities Asha Deep puts a lot of focus on providing people with intellectual impairments with the tools they need to carry out Activities of Daily Living (ADL). These fundamental living skills include duties including maintaining personal hygiene, preparing meals, and communicating, allowing individuals to live more independently.

2. Academics That Work: To meet each person's unique requirements, the institute offers academic functional training. This comprises reading, numeracy, and other cognitive abilities that enable persons to interact meaningfully with the outside world.

3. Prevocational Exercises Asha Deep involves its clients in prevocational programmes because it understands the value

of vocational skills. These activities help people develop self-reliance and financial independence while preparing them for potential work prospects.

4. Music and Sports at Asha Deep promotes participation in sports and music programmes for people with disabilities in collaboration with groups like Special Olympics Bharat. These extracurricular activities foster collaboration, physical health, and personal development.

• **Non-academic pursuits:**

1. Rehabilitation for mental health: Rehabilitation of homeless people with mental health issues is a big element of Asha Deep's goal. In order to assist these people in regaining stability and reintegrating into society, the organisation offers psychiatric care, therapy, and assistance.

2. Initiatives for community-based mental health: Through community outreach programmes for mental health, Asha Deep has increased its reach. These initiatives seek to debunk the stigma around mental illness and increase public understanding of mental health services.

3. The Resource Centre For persons with disabilities and their families, the centre serves as a central hub of resources, offering helpful advice, counselling, and assistance. It acts as a network of support, providing aid outside of traditional academic or clinical activity.

The Asha Deep Foundation, a non-profit company that has been working on development projects in many Indian states for more than 40 years, including Delhi, Mumbai, and Chennai, includes the Asha Deep Rehabilitation Centre in Patna. The facility, which is always working to improve the quality of life for people with disabilities, has come to be seen as a representation of development and inclusion in the area.

Patna's Asha Deep Rehabilitation Centre is more than simply a school; it is a haven for growth and hope. It has changed the lives of numerous people with intellectual impairments and mental health issues via its academic and extracurricular activities, providing them the ability and confidence to lead more fulfilled lives. The centre is a shining example of compassion and devotion in the area of disability services because of its dedication to education, rehabilitation, and community assistance.

- **Programmes for Divyang Children**
- The idea of inclusive education is an important concept in the field of education. It refers to the practice of providing education to all students, regardless of their abilities or disabilities, in an environment that is conducive to their learning and development. One way in which inclusion education can be achieved is through special schools.
- Special schools are educational establishments that serve the needs of students with disabilities or unique educational needs. These schools provide specialized instruction, support, and services to help students reach their full potential. In addition to academic instruction, special schools may offer therapies such as speech and language therapy, occupational therapy, and physical therapy, as well as assistive technology and other accommodations to meet the individual needs of students.

- While the concept of special schools may seem at odds with the idea of inclusive education, these schools can actually play an important role in promoting inclusion. By providing specialized instruction and support to students with special needs, special schools can help these students overcome barriers to learning and achieve success. The success can then translate to greater inclusion in mainstream settings, as students gain confidence and skills that allow them to participate more fully in academic and social activities.
- Moreover, special schools can also serve as a model for inclusive practices. By providing a supportive and inclusive environment for students with special needs, special schools can demonstrate the value of inclusion and inspire other educational institutions to adopt similar practices. In this way, special schools can help to promote a culture of inclusion throughout the entire education system.
- The present study is a case study on 'Asha Deep Rehabilitation Centre for Divyangjan'. This institution is a school for children with special needs which is situated in Patna. The purpose of the study is to examine and assess the learning experiences gained by children with special needs at Asha Deep Rehabilitation Centre for Divyangjan.The study aimed to explore how this centre for rehabilitation has helped to lead the children with special needs into the mainstream of society and to assess how this institution is promoting a culture of inclusion and helping

children to be valuable members of the inclusive society.

- **Programmes organized for Hearing Impaired**

Asha Deep Rehabilitation Center for Divyangjan's Hearing Impairment Department hosts several hearing-related events. The section offers early intervention and rehabilitation to detect and treat hearing issues. Pre-school teaching helps hearing-impaired kids learn school skills. Hearing-impaired people also get speech therapy. Computer training helps hearing-impaired people become more employable. The Hearing Impairment section of Asha Deep Rehabilitation Center for Divyangjan helps hearing-impaired peopleto communicate and attain their full potential.

- **ProgrammesOrganised for Children who are Intellectually Challenged**

Activities at Asha Deep Rehabilitation Center for Divyangjan enable intellectually differently abled people learn self-help and enhance their quality of life. The institution teaches lunchtime activities, dressing, irritation control, and entire and optimum motor functions. The facility also helps preschoolers with speech, language, reading, writing, and math. Intellectually disabled people also learn social and communication skills to engage with others. Sports, dance, and vocational training give exercise and skill-building in addition to intellectual and social growth. Asha Deep Rehabilitation Center for Divyangjan helps intellectually disabled people live fulfilled lives by providing a variety of activities and training.

- **Programms organized by the Hearing and Visual Impaired**

Asha Deep Rehabilitation Center for Divyangjan serves hearing and visually impaired people in its Hearing and Sight Impaired Department. After the lockdown due to Covid 19 Pandemic, the Department of visual impaired session was closed due to a lack of funds. The department still arranges teacher home visits for hearing and visually impaired students.

- ***Curricular Activities***

Asha Deep Rehabilitation Centre for Divyangjan has a well-planned and well-organized academic calendar that helps it to achieve its objectives successfully every year. The instruction process is in Hindi language. The followscurricular activities are done.

(i) The centre takes care that every child develops reading and writing skills.

(ii) Sign language is the medium of communication between students and teachers.

(iii) The centre makes sure that in the very first three years, the students are acquitted with the sign language that will help the child in his personal growth and academic growth.

(iv) It follows the regular textbooks from class first onwards just as they are followed in any other normal rehabilitation centre curriculum.

(v) English, Hindi, Mathematics, Science, Social Science, General Knowledge, Drawing, and Sports all these subjects are given a place in its general weekly timetable.

(vi) Normally the rehabilitation centre is following the Bihar Board books in their curriculum and prepares the students for any general competitive examination.

- **Co-Curricular Activities**

Co-curricular Activities are part of the holistic development of a child but mostly it is seen that parents give more pressure on studies or academic performance than co-curricular activities. As narrated by the teachers, parents of children with special needs do not encourage outdoor games after rehabilitation centre. They undervalue after-rehabilitation centre activities for their special needs children. Many times, most of the time is spent on academics or therapies or they do not feel the need for extracurricular activities, so there is a good chance that the parents undermine the child and rob the child of opportunities for growth and social being.

Assembly:

The day in the rehabilitation Centre begins with a general assembly.

The assembly starts with a drill. It is followed by a prayer. The daily news is read by one of the students.The news is transmitted in sign language by one of their teachers. The assembly concludes with the singing of the national anthem which is sung by the students in sign language.

To give priority to the all-around development of the child, the institute conducts the following activities as part of the co-curricular activities which are as follows:

(i) Art and craft

(ii) Aerobics

(iii) Yoga
(iv) Dance
(v) Sports
(vi) Gardening
(vii) Drawing
(viii) Painting
(ix) Different competitions
(x) Educational Tours
(xi) Mime
(xii) Computer Training
(xiii) Visit to Museum
(xiv) Visit to a Bank
(xv) Visit to Railway Station and understand the necessary things
(xvi) Visit to a Market
(xvii) Celebration of different Festivals
(xviii) Annual Cultural Programme

The Centre takes care of the personal growth of the child and helps them to understand the integrity of life. Children enjoy these programmes to their best and take part in the way they can participate. Teachers guide the students to dance even if they are not able to hear the music. Children take part in sports even when they are not able to see.

Extracurricular activities have the possibilities to open the possibility of children mixing up with others. They increase their faith in each other and become friends. They start social interaction which helps them in their growth. As we know children with special needs have communication challenges at the early stage of life. So, mixing and communicating helps the children in their growth. This mixing takes place because the children meet with each other in a very different way and in a very different environment.

- **Activities related to the life skills development of students of Asha Deep Rehabilitation Centre for Divyangjan**

Asha Deep Rehabilitation Centre for Divyangjan takes care of the children's life skill training programme too. Life skill training programmes are designed to provide adequate useful skills to the children so that they can take part according to their interests outside rehabilitation centre hours. It helps them to keep themselves busy in their own interest programme so that they do not feel out of place. The acquisition of skills is always of great importance, as it can provide a good source of income too. The main goal of such programmes is to teach children to be self-sufficient. Life skills help children to survive to reach adulthood and become self-supporting individuals who partially can care for themselves without being totally dependent on others. Children also to some extent become more responsible to take care of themselves and their families. They contribute significantly to the future of their own community by their own contribution. So, such learning will always open a way for the child to provide for themselves and will enable them to be less dependent on others.

Asha Deep Rehabilitation Centre for Divyangjan also trains children to face the world with dignity. Life skills training programme is conducted for hearing-impaired children to have a significant effect on the social skills of the students.

It also helps in self-awareness, cooperation, assertion, and self-control.

Some of the activities used to teach life skills to the children of Asha Deep Rehabilitation Centre for Divyangjan are as follows:

(i) Self-introduction

(ii) Analysis and solving every day's classroom problems

(iii) Awareness of one's behaviour in a particular event or situation

(iv) Completing puzzles in groups or individually

(v) Role play

(vi) Mime

All these help the children in their personal growth, and it opens the door for the children to shine in the world. The child feels worthy of his own existence and takes care of his own personal needs.

- **Activities related to the vocational development of students of Asha Deep Rehabilitation Centre for Divyangjan.**

Asha Deep Rehabilitation Centre for Divyangjan does not only take care of the academics of the children but also takes care of vocational training too. Different categories of children with special needs come here, but not all are able to clear their normal curriculum studies. They are taken care of in a different way so that they too are able to take care of themselves and their family's needs in long run. Keeping this in mind vocational training is also a part of the co-curricular activities of Asha Deep Rehabilitation Centre for Divyangjan. Vocational training for intellectually disabled children in Asha Deep Rehabilitation Centre for Divyangjan is as follows:

(i) Computer programme

(ii) Data entry Programme

(iii) Candle Making

(iv) Envelop Making

(v) Key Rings Making

- **Conclusion**

The study was conducted to get a detailed study on Asha Deep Rehabilitation Centre for Divyangjan and to analyse and assess how much the Centre is successful in creating a supportive and inclusive learning environment for all students studying there. Education for children with special needs of every age is a big challenge to society. In this context, the researcher has done a case study on Asha Deep Rehabilitation Centre for Divyangjan. The views of the parents and the students were assessed to see how the rehabilitation centre is helping the children in their personal growth. The study also aimed to see that after reaching a certain age, where are these children placed in life so that they could live and grow in society and lead a dignified life independently. The perception and views of the parents and students towards the rehabilitation centre were analysed. The different objectives that gave a proper direction to the study helped in drawing the conclusion.

Chapter 3
Enrollment and Retention

- Enrolment and retention of students
- Demographical territory of beneficiaries
- Religious-wise beneficiaries

- **Enrollment and Retention of Students**

After the analysis of the essential documents related to admission, dropouts and the total number of students, data was obtained which is shown in Table 3.1.

Table 3.1

Enrollment and Retention of Students of Asha Deep Rehabilitation Center for Divyangjan

Year	No. of Students	New Admission	Drop out	Completed Class VIII	Completed Class X	Total No. of Students
2010	134	42	17	13	-	146
2011	146	52	15	16	-	167
2012	167	47	23	14	-	177
2013	177	30	18	17	-	172
2014	172	47	19	9	-	191
2015	191	44	21	16	-	198
2016	198	29	18	15	-	194
2017	194	47	26	14	-	201
2018	201	44	21	8	-	216
2019	216	60	28	Continued Class IX	-	248
2020	248	-	-	Continued Class IX	-	248
2021	248	22	59	-	22	189
2022	242	53	-	-		242

Asha Deep Rehabilitation Center for Divyangjan educates and rehabilitates children with disabilities. Its success depends on student enrolment and retention. Table 3.1 illustrates that student's enrolment increases annually. The table shows dropouts are also there because far-flung children couldn't reach the school in time and parents also had difficulty to reach them daily. Some parents were also dissatisfied with their children's progress because they expected a fast change in their behaviour, which was not happening. When they reach class IX, dropout rates dropped as children and parents found stability at the institute.

- **Demographical Territory of Beneficiaries.**

Table 3.2 shows the district-wise distribution of the beneficiaries of Asha Deep Rehabilitation Center for Divyangjan during the year 2021-22.

Table 3.2

Demographical Territory of Beneficiaries

Sr. No.	District	Number	Percentage
1.	Patna	55	22.72
2.	East Champaran	16	6.61
3.	Nawada	07	2.89
4.	Vaishali	06	2.48
5.	Begusarai	06	2.48
6.	West Champaran	13	5.37
7.	Gaya	06	2.48
8.	Jehanabad	07	2.89
9.	Bhojpur (Ara)	08	3.31
10.	Buxar	05	2.07
11.	Gopalganj	09	3.72
12.	Saran	09	3.72
13.	Muzaffarpur	08	3.31
14.	Nalanda	06	2.48
15.	Jamui	06	2.48
16.	Munger	08	3.31
17.	Darbhanga	10	4.13
18.	Bhagalpur	06	2.48
19.	Sitamarhi	06	2.48
20.	Madhepura	04	1.65
21.	Madhubani	05	2.07
22.	Aurangabad	09	3.72
23.	Supaul	12	4.95
24.	Arwal	03	1.24
25.	Saharsa	06	2.48
26.	Any Other	06	2.48
	Total	**242**	**100**

Table 3.2 shows that 22.72 % of students who studies in Asha Deep Rehabilitation Centre belong to Patna district which is the highest among all the other districts of Bihar.East Champaran follows with 6.61 % and West Champaran stands in third place with 5.37 % of students studying in the Rehabilitation centre. Students from these three districts top the distribution with 33.88 % of students in total studying in Asha Deep. The rest students are from the rest of the districts of Bihar. Out of 242 students, 133 (54.96 %) students are from only 9 districts of Bihar. The rest are from other 29 districts of Bihar.

- **Religious-wise beneficiaries**

Table 3.3 shows the religion-wise distribution of the beneficiaries of Asha Deep Rehabilitation Center for Divyangjan during the year 2021-22.

Table 3.3

Beneficiaries of Asha Deep Rehabilitation Center for Divyangjan based on Religion.

Sr. No.	Religion	Number	Percentage
1.	Hindus	198	81.81
2.	Muslims	42	17.35
3.	Sikhs	00	00
4.	Christian	02	0.82
5.	Any Other	00	0
	Total	**242**	**100**

Table 3.3 shows the religion-wise demographical territory of Asha Deep Rehabilitation centre, Patna which shows that 81.81 % of students are Hindus and are the biggest

beneficiaries in the Rehabilitation Centre. It was noted that in the census 2011, in the state of Bihar, the percentage of Hindus is 82.69, Muslims 16.87, and Christians 0.12. Similar data is reflected in Table 4.3 which shows that 17.35 % of the beneficiaries are Muslims, and 0.82% are Christians. The sample is a true representation of Bihar. Being a Christian minority institution Asha Deep Rehabilitation centre, Patna cares about the representation of all religions.

Chapter 4
Infrastructure and Facilities

- Medical facilities provided by the institute
- Infrastructural facilities

- **Medical Facilities provided by the Institute**

Children with special needs get medical treatment at Asha Deep Rehabilitation Centre for Divyangjan. Speech therapy aids speech and language development. Also, a psychologist provides emotional support and counselling to children and their families. Play therapy supports differently abled youngsters. The clinic offers a psychiatrist for more complicated mental health issues. The centre also conducts medical camps and follow-ups for differently abled people. Asha Deep Rehabilitation Centre for Divyangjan helps differently abled people stay healthy by giving these medical services.

- **Medical Facilities in Asha Deep**

Medical facilities at Asha Deep Rehabilitation Centre for Divyangjan

i Speech therapy

ii Paediatrician

iii Psychologist

iv Play Therapy

v Psychiatrist

vi Medical Camps and follow-ups

- **Infrastructural Facilities**

Asha Deep Rehabilitation Centre for Divyangjan's facility includes everything pupils need. Classrooms with smart boards and student-friendly furnishings help pupils study. The restrooms are gender-specific and accommodate unique needs. A large multipurpose hall hosts indoor games, cultural events, and other activities. The school contains a library and computer lab. Daily yoga and morning assembly are held in the school playground. Prayer, National Anthem, and physical training follow the gathering. Sign language is used for most activities so that deaf and dumb children may follow the activities.

- **Infrastructure of Asha Deep Rehabilitation Center for Divyangjan.**

Table 4.1

Infrastructure details of Asha Deep Rehabilitation Center for Divyangjan

Sr. No.	Rooms	Number
1.	Classrooms	12 Old + 6 New = 18
2.	Staff Room	01
3.	Toilets	Boys 12Girls 12
4.	Auditorium	01
5.	Any Other	Computer Lab Smart Class Library Storeroom Science Lab Auditorium

Table 4.1 shows the details of the infrastructure of the Asha Deep Rehabilitation Centre for Divyangjan. It can be inferred that the necessary facilities are available for its students studying here. Well-equipped classrooms with smart boards and furniture in the classroom are student friendly which provides the students with an ambience to study well. There are separate toilets for girls and boys and it was observed that the need of special children was taken care in designing the toilets. There is a big multipurpose hall where various indoor games competitions, cultural programmes and various activities are conducted. The rehabilitation centre has a well- equipped computer lab and library with books for students. There is a playground in which they have yoga and morning assembly every day. During the assembly physical training is also given. Most of the activities are done in sign language so that children with hearing impairment can comprehend and participate.

Chapter 5
Financial Condition

- Financial condition of the institution

A self-financed institution, Asha Deep Rehabilitation Center for Divyangjan is supported by the tuition fee payments made by the parents of the students enrolled there. The school administration finds it very challenging to give their instructors a good salary due to the small amount of payment received from the pupils, which is a major obstacle in finding qualified teachers who could care for the children with special needs.

Chapter 6
Contribution to Creating Inclusion in Society

- Inclusive Education and Constitutional Role
- Background of the Inclusive Education Programme
- Problems and Challenges of Inclusive Education
- From Special Education to Inclusion
- Contribution of Asha Deep Rehabilitation Center for Divyangjan to create inclusion in society

• Inclusive Education and Constitutional Role

Inclusive Education can benefit children who have learning disabilities, mild or borderline intellectual functioning, and other children with disabilities. Some schools have adapted a separate way of assessing these children instead of the usual way of assessments. The oral assessment is given priorities, and projects these children can understand and do easily are given. Many times, some experimental methods of learning are also used for their training. Activities are designed in such a way that they take care of the co-curricular assessments that benefit these children. Schools even provide unique resource rooms with trained resource instructors and adequate learning aids that make it possible for these children to grow incredibly positively. All schools should make these facilities compulsory to ensure they adapt to inclusive education.

- As we see the availability of abundant opportunities across different fields, be it music, sports, martial arts, art, and craft, children with disabilities can excel across multiple myriad areas with basic academics and adequate life skills. Different TV channels organize other talent shows in which these children participate in various capacities and have touched many hearts present in the shows. It has often been seen that they do much better than any average child. This gives a clear message to society that if these children are given proper training and platform, there are chances they can excel on their own. This is the right way where the current education system of our country needs to focus on empowering children with disabilities.
- Many Inclusive school communities have educational settings that provide students with disabilities to have equal opportunities to participate and receive support in different aspects of school life alongside peers who do not have disabilities. In an inclusive system, there are exceptional educators the need specialized instructional support personnel, general educators, and other education personnel to work together to take care of the needs of the students with disabilities. This opens the door for collaboration with these educators for better support and learning. This also gives an opportunity for the students to participate and develop their talents. The research demonstrates that a learning community is called to be better, richer, and more

effective than helping disabled students fully participate in learning and development.

- The Directive Principles of the Indian Constitution, the National Policy of Education (NPE-1986), The RCI Act, the Persons with Disabilities Act (1996, 2016), and The Sarva Shiksha Abhiyan (SSA 2010), all of them ensure equality for disabled children. They all speak of empowering children to guarantee admission, retention, and education of all children aged 6 to 14 years, including the disabled ones. This is an assurance that no normal school can deny admission to any disabled child in any circumstances.

- The precedent for inclusive education was set in the Least Restrictive Environment (LRE) clause of Public Law 94-142, originally passed by Congress in 1975. The recent version of the law for the disabled is known as the Individuals with Disabilities Education Act (IDEA) which came into force in 2004. In the meantime, many strides have been made in realizing the law's intent, which often helps schools still treat inclusive education. This is a big challenge that supports students with disabilities. We often find that separateness and exclusion can be defined in the educational experience, particularly for the students with the most significant cognitive disabilities. The slow rate of implementation and the received challenges involving different educators, students, and their families have been found to be many compelling reasons to support inclusive education for students with and without disabilities.

- We see that education is a fundamental human right, and ensuring that all can realize their ability and potential is essential. The main key aim of education is to give all citizens the necessary skills and different values to improve their quality of life and standard of living. These aims can be achieved when we can continue to work together to improve access to education and to provide a better quality of educational facilities equitably.

- Inclusion in education involves diversity and recognizes the value of human living. It provides a sense of belonging for every child and their family. It also gives an acceptance of individuality in diversity and different opportunities to all the children who are involved in the curriculum that teaches them and helps them in learning. Every child that attends the school is engaged in general education in a classroom day today and is involved in learning. These students naturally support and help each other understand and overcome the different daily life routine challenges. These students are grouped in different groups and are involved in various classroom activities, making the structure more open and flexible. This also gives the group to enhance the individual ability and respect it. Naturally, we also find that the group of students help each other, and they are presumed to be competent. All of them are incredibly supportive of each other in curriculum adaptation and differentiated teaching activities. This group of students is given equal opportunity and so they are known and valued as full members of the school community. They develop meaningful social relationships with their peers and participate in different aspects of their school life. We also find them connected in social media platforms where they act and experience like normal individuals.Many apps are made user-friendly and these children with disabilities participate by using them as active interaction platforms like any other normal person without a disability.

- In the school system, Inclusive education adopts a process where strategic plans and policies are adapted. These plans and strategies help to improve and change the teaching strategies for a broader and more diverse range of children who can be taken care of and given proper training. This also helps the families of children with disabilities. Inclusive education implicitly means identifying the child's needs and learning style and adapting the classroom in such a way that the teaching strategies are to ensure high-quality learning outcomes. These outcomes are helpful for all children in the class.
- The United Nations' contribution is very much counted in the field of imparting and caring for the education of disabled children. The United Nations Educational, Scientific and Cultural Organisation (UNESCO) defines inclusive education as a process that responds to every student's life. It also speaks of increasing the children's life and

participation and reducing exclusion within and from education. It emphasizes the child's attendance, involvement in learning, and achievement. It gives focuses on those children, especially those who are excluded due to different reasons and those who are at risk of being marginalized.

- It constitutes an essential element to advance on the EFA agenda. The concept of education for all does not imply the concept of inclusion. Being intended to ensure access to education, inclusion involves access to high-quality education without any discrimination of any kind, within or outside of the school system. This teaching requires an in-depth transformation of the education system prevailing in today's day-to-day life. We must accept that without inclusion, certain groups of students are likely to be excluded from the everyday activity of social life. Inclusion should be a guiding force and principle that directs our educational policies and programmes so that education can be for all and not only for the majority.
- The National Policy of Education (NEP) created and came into force in 1986 also gave importance to inclusion in the school system. This was followed by the Integrated Education of Disabled Children (IEDC, 1974), which helped the children to be included in the mainstream of the classrooms. It then spoke of children with 'mild' disabilities should be made part of the mainstream of the classroom. In contrast, children with 'moderate to

severe' disabilities should be placed in segregated special schools that will mainly take care of their needs. The Action Programme of 1992 was also created to implement the guidelines of NPE-1986 stating taking care of special needs children. Broadening the sense and the NPE's definitions of who should be included in the mainstream of schooling and who should not. It defined that the children with a disability to whom it's possible to be educated in the general schools should not be admitted to the special school and should be part of the normal school system. It also spoke of the children by saying that once children with disabilities acquire basic living skills, which would be learned in resource rooms or special schools, they should be admitted into the mainstream education system.

- In the year 1992, we also see the year of the Rehabilitation Council of India (RCI) Act. The RCI Act provides standards for rehabilitation professionals; one type of rehabilitation professional is a special education teacher. In the year 2002, the 86th amendment of the constitution was made that mandated free and compulsory education to all children ages 6-14 and with the help of the World Bank, the Government of India gave a start to Sarva Shiksha Abhiyan – SSA that spoke of Education for all in India.
- The Right to Education Act was framed as a 'social justice and collective advocacy perspective' rather than through a framework of individual rights, it is

not disability-specific but inclusive of children with disabilities, with specific sections that address the educational rights of students with disabilities. The RTE act was passed in 2009 and fully effected in 2010.

- It was becoming important that our country create a bill around sections 45 and 21 (A) of the constitution that will become the Right to Education Act originally floated in 2005. This was the same year when the Ministry of Human Resource Development also drafted the Action Plan for the Inclusion Education of Children and Youth with Disabilities (IECYD). This action plan envisioned that all children with special needs would have access to mainstream education. The government specifically collaborated between the Rehabilitation Council and the National Council for Teachers Education to facilitate this plan. It was mainly to ensure adequate numbers of teachers trained to care for these special children's needs in inclusive education. This ensured that proper physical and ideological infrastructure facilitated inclusion in schools. This plan specifically moved from integration towards inclusion, stating that under the Scheme of Integrated Education of Disabled Children (IEDC) as it stands in the present form. Children with special needs are placed in regular schools without making any changes in the school to accommodate and support diverse needs. The revised IECYD will, in contrast, modify the existing physical infrastructures and teaching methodologies to meet the needs of all children, including children with Special Needs.

- The Commission, at its fifty-eighth session, adapted resolution 58/4 of 22nd May 2002 on promoting an inclusive, a barrier-free, and rights-based society for people with disabilities in the Asian and Pacific region in the twenty-first century, by which it proclaimed the extension of the Asian and Pacific Decade of Disabled Persons, 1993-2002, for another decade, 2003-2012 Biwako Millennium Framework (1993-2012).

- **Background of the Inclusive Education Programme**

The Indian government is constitutionally obliged to ensure every kid has access to basic education. Since India's independence in 1947, the government has enacted several regulations relating to special education. The Integrated Education for Disabled Children (IEDC) plan of 1974 was one of the first formal efforts made by the Government of India (NCERT, 2011). During the post-independence period, the Kothari Commission (1966) emphasized the significance of teaching children with impairments (Pandey 2006). The Ministry of Welfare of the Government of India recognized the critical need for an organization to oversee and control HRD programmes in disability rehabilitation in the 1980s. 90% of India's estimated 40 million children aged four to sixteen years with physical and mental impairments were excluded from mainstream school until the 1990s. The National Policy on Education (NPE, 1986) and the Programme of Action (1992) both emphasise integrating special needs students with other groups. In 1994–95, the Indian government launched the District

Primary Education Project (DPEP). Inclusive education was incorporated into the District Primary Education Program in the late 1990s (i.e., in 1997). (DPEP). In accordance with global trends, this programme placed a specific emphasis on integrating children with mild to moderate impairments. It became one of the GOI's most extensive flagship programmes at the time, with a budget of 40,000 million rupees (approximately 740 million US dollars). One such programme is the Sarva Shiksha Abhiyan (SSA), established in 2001 to accomplish the Universalization of Elementary Education objective. Access, enrolment, and retention of all children aged 6 to 14 are three key aspects of UEE. Under the SSA, a zero-rejection policy has been implemented, ensuring that every child with Special Needs (CWSN) receives a relevant and excellent education regardless of the kind, category, or degree of impairment. The 2005 National Curriculum Framework (NCF) established a clear framework for inclusive education. A National Action Plan for the inclusion of children and teenagers with disabilities in school was adapted by the Ministry of Human Resource Development in 2005. In 2009-10, IEDC was renamed "Inclusive Education of the Handicapped at the Secondary Stage (IEDSS)" to help the inclusive education of disabled pupils in 9th and 10th. Since 2013, this plan has been absorbed into the Rashtriya Madhyamik Shiksha Abhiyan (RMSA). Integrating these youngsters into regular classrooms is critical to help them socialize and gain confidence.

- **Problems and Challenges of Inclusive Education**
    - The number of children with special needs in India is enormous; their issues are complicated,

resources are few, and societal attitudes are harmful. The path to inclusive education is long and winding, with many obstacles and possibilities along the way. India is a multilingual, multicultural, and multireligious country whose people are divided along socioeconomic and caste lines. India is the world's second-most populous country, behind China, with an estimated population of 1,210 million. It is home to 17% of the world's population and 20% of the world's unschooled youngsters. The goal of inclusion is to support kids. As schools accommodate kids with more diverse origins and skills, the primary goal has grown more difficult. The number of persons with disabilities in India is estimated to be 26 million, or about 2.1 percent of the overall population, according to official figures from the Census of India (Government of India, 2011). However, according to UNICEF's Report on the Status of Disability in India (2000), about 30 million children in India are disabled in some way. Approximately 10% of the world's population has a disability, with 80 percent living in poor nations. However, in India, 75 percent of persons with disabilities reside in rural regions. Since the country's independence, the government has enacted a number of policies concerning special education. There may be several obstacles to educating students with impairments in conventional classrooms. These difficulties might be caused by a lack of appropriate human and financial resources, unfavourable teacher and community attitudes, and non-disabled classmates and their parents. Despite the Indian government's attempts to develop policies inclusive of persons with disabilities, its implementation efforts have not resulted in an inclusive educational system. Furthermore, the number of children dropping out of school is increasing, particularly in low-income communities. Due to their parent's financial difficulties, students are compelled to drop out of school and labour to assist their parents to make ends meet. As a result, the number of child laborers is increasing, resulting in physical and psychological problems. Negative attitudes and behaviour on the part of both instructors and parents with respect to the ability of handicapped children to learn to pose unique problems. Another significant issue is that most handicapped individuals continue to be denied equitable access to mainstream schooling.

- In India, large class sizes offer another obstacle to implementing inclusive education. In order to teach children with disabilities in inclusive education settings, Das, Kuyini, and Desai (2013) looked at the existing skill levels of normal primary and secondary school instructors in Delhi, India. They discovered that over 70% of normal school instructors had no special education training and had no prior experience teaching kids with impairments. In addition, 87% of instructors lacked access to support services in their classes. According to the Sixth All India Educational Survey (NCERT, 1998), special needs education is required for about 20 million of India's 200 million school-aged children (6–14 years). Even though the national average for gross enrolment in school is above 90%, only about 5% of children with disabilities attend school. For children with impairments, peer acceptance is a much more complex problem. Children with disabilities are frequently ridiculed and harassed by their classmates who are not handicapped. A high percentage of disabled children live in households with incomes much below the poverty line.

- In India, most school employees are unprepared to plan and administer educational programmes for kids with disabilities in normal schools. In India, most teacher education programmes do not include a disability studies course. In India, most schools are poorly constructed, and just a few are prepared to accommodate the special requirements of disabled children. It is also worth mentioning that obtaining and resourcing assistive equipment presents problems.
- Despite many attempts in India to promote inclusive education, around 94 percent of children with disabilities were denied access to educational programmes. Over and beyond some of the problems that India has in common with other developing nations, certain unique characteristics will make educational reform

extremely difficult to achieve. The Government of India's commitment to the Universalisation of Elementary Education (UEE) would not be completely realised until the special educational needs of physically and mentally challenged children are addressed.

- Inclusion is becoming a buzzword in education circles, but there are still many misconceptions about it. We find a lack of confidence in the teachers to teach in inclusive settings. The main reason is that they are mostly not equipped with the latest updated given situation so that they are able to adapt it in their teaching. Many teachers are not trained well to deal with inclusive education. Many teacher training institutions do not support the training in such a manner that the trainees have exposure to the need of special children. Many teachers cannot handle the methodology suited to the educational needs of children with special needs. As we find that the training lacks steps to be taken care of the needy students with special needs the curriculum is not designed in such a way that can cater to their needs. This is a major problem as the curriculum is not according to the time the children cannot be guided by the teachers helping the children with their needs. Community plays an important role in all this and many times, the community itself is not incredibly supportive. So, the problem of mobilizing the community to participate in inclusive education programme is the need of the hour.

- An important step taken through legislation is the Right to Persons with special needs Act 2016. This act aimed at reducing the discrimination experienced by the divyangjan. Disability is generally equated with incapacity and inability to do something. There is a widespread underestimation of the abilities and potential of divyangjan due to the general public perception that has a prejudiced mind to keep judging. These minds create a vicious cycle of underachievement and think that children with special needs cannot do anything in life. We often underestimate the abilities and potential of the divyangjan due to general public perception and prejudices. Many times, we create a vicious cycle of underachievement of our ability. We need to try to understand their capabilities and achievement. This impact keeps them far from life experiences as we fail to give them opportunities to show their talents and abilities. We always try to keep them in our helping arms and behave as they need us. We also think they are help seekers even without understanding their feelings. We try to keep them very protective as they always like to stand independently and do whatever they wish. If we guide them properly and think of their vocational rehabilitation, it can be incredibly positive and useful for them. Training in proper time and guidance will make them in person more functional and psychologically strong and develop their inner ability. They also develop in their emotional impairments or health disabilities to overcome barriers that help them grow properly. As we take care of their vocational rehabilitation the divyangjan depends on the psychosocial approach that takes care of every individual in different ways. Every child develops in their individual way in the context of the combined influence that the psychological factors and the surroundings of their social environment have on their physical and mental wellness and growth that helps their ability to function. At times, persons may not be fully aware of the relationship between their mental and emotional well-being and the environment. So, everything must be taken care of when discussing children with special care and special needs.

- Rights are interconnected and interdependent. In the absence of one, it becomes difficult to enjoy other rights. Despite recognition by the international community of the dignity of human life, Divyangjan has remained marginalized and excluded from participating in different aspects of community life. They have always been perceived as lacking the abilities and potential to engage in any meaningful activity or work. In India, The Right to Persons with Disabilities Act of 2016 adopts a multi-prone approach to the issue of employment of Divyangjan.
- In order to promote the employment of Divyangjan in the organized formal sector, it provides for a scheme of quota to the extent of

4% in all government departments (Central and State government), public sector undertakings, and local authorities to be distributed equally to the extent of 1% each among persons suffering from blindness and low vision, persons suffering from hearing impairment, and persons suffering from a locomotor disability or cerebral palsy (Section 33)

- **From Special Education to Inclusion**

Special schools are educational institutions that cater to the needs of students with special needs or impairments. To enable pupils to realise their best potential, these schools offer specialised instruction, assistance, and services. Special schools may provide therapies, including speech and language therapy, occupational therapy, and physical therapy in addition to academic education, as well as assistive technology and other modifications to fit each student's unique needs.

- Although the idea of special schools may appear incompatible with that of inclusive education, these institutions can help foster inclusion. Special schools can assist students with special needs to overcome obstacles to learning and succeeding by offering them customised teaching and assistance. When students gain self-assurance and abilities that enable them to participate more completely in academic and social activities, their success can result in greater inclusion in more mainstream settings.

- Moreover, special schools can also serve as a model for inclusive practices. Special schools can show the value of inclusion and encourage other educational institutions to follow similar methods by offering a friendly and inclusive atmosphere for kids with special needs. This is one way that special schools can support the development of an inclusive culture throughout the entire educational system.
- Ultimately, inclusive education aims to provide all students with the opportunity to reach their full potential, and special schools can be an important part of achieving this goal.

- **Contribution of Asha Deep Rehabilitation Center for Divyangjan to create inclusion in society**

Asha Deep Rehabilitation Center for Divyangjan encourages social inclusion. To foster inclusivity, the centre offers athletics, drawing, painting, dance, and karate for kids. These activities help differently abled kids socialise and learn new abilities. Differently-abled students experience Christmas celebrations with other kids at the institution. This removes obstacles to disability-related social inclusion. Whenever possible hearing-impaired children also socialize. This fosters mutual learning and friendship. The Asha Deep Rehabilitation Center for Divyangjan allows persons with disabilities to engage in the community, enabling a sense of belonging and breaking down barriers.

Asha Deep Rehabilitation Center for Divyangjan offers rehabilitation treatments to people with impairments.

Through a number of initiatives, the organisation has significantly aided in the inclusion of people with disabilities in society, including:

Asha Deep offers vocational training and skill development to people with impairments so they may become independent and self-sufficient. This not only enables them to support themselves but it also increases their self-confidence and aids in their social integration.

Asha Deep runs awareness initiatives in schools, universities, and communities to make people more understanding of individuals with disabilities. This fosters a more inclusive society and lessens the stigma and prejudice experienced by people with disabilities.

Infrastructure that is accessible: Asha Deep is an advocate for infrastructure that is accessible, including access roads, buildings, and public areas. Because of this, it is simpler for people with disabilities to move about and participate in neighborhood activities.

Asha Deep advocates for the rights of people with disabilities by working with the government and other groups. This involves promoting legislation, legal reforms, and the adoption of practises and policies that accommodate people with disabilities.

In India, the Asha Deep Rehabilitation Center for Divyangjan has contributed to developing a more inclusive society for people with disabilities. Through their initiatives, people with disabilities have gained more agency, stigma and discrimination have decreased, and accessibility and inclusivity have been promoted.

Like many other institutions, Asha Deep Rehabilitation Center for Divyangjan struggled with the COVID-19 outbreak. The organisation took many steps to protect the children with special needs during the epidemic. All precautions, like sanitising facilities, handwashing, and using masks, were taken. The online classes were provided to the students, and notes were shared through WhatsApp in PDF documents and Videos. Throughout the COVID-19 epidemic, Asha Deep Rehabilitation Center for Divyangjan demonstrated its dedication to the safety, well-being, and ongoing care of people with disabilities and their families.

- **Conclusion**

Many nations' constitutions, like that of India's, recognize the right to inclusive education as one of the most essential human rights. It maintains the ideal of equality by ensuring that all children, irrespective of their talents or impairments, have access to education of a high standard. The duty of the constitution is to protect this right and encourage education systems that are inclusive, with the end goal of creating a more equal society. The Right to Education Act of 2009, which was passed in India, encourages inclusive education in an explicit manner.

The transition from conventional, segregated education to a more inclusive approach that includes kids with disabilities in regular classrooms is exemplified by the inclusive education program, which reflects a change away from traditional education. It works toward the goal of establishing an educational setting that is welcoming to children of varying abilities and provides them with helpful resources.

There are several obstacles in the way of inclusive education, including a lack of suitable infrastructure, insufficient teacher training, and the need for specialized assistance for kids who have a variety of different requirements. Conquering these obstacles is very necessary in order to make inclusive education efficient and fair for everyone involved.

There has been a substantial paradigm change in how people with disabilities are educated, and it may be characterized by the movement away from special education and toward inclusion. It encourages the integration and involvement of children with special needs in regular classes, which in turn fosters an educational climate that is more welcoming of diversity and has a wider range of perspectives.

Along with a large number of other organizations, the Asha Deep Rehabilitation Center for Divyangjan plays an important part in the effort to increase social inclusion. It does this by providing assistance to people with disabilities in the areas of education and social integration, so helping to the creation of a society that is more equal and welcoming to those with differing abilities.

Chapter 7
Approach Adopted during COVID-19 Pandemic

- Approach adopted by Asha Deep Rehabilitation Center for Divyangjan during the COVID-19 pandemic

Asha Deep Rehabilitation Center for Divyangjan struggled with the COVID-19 outbreak like many other institutions. The organisation took many steps to protect the children with special needs during the epidemic. All precautions were taken like sanitizing facilities, handwashing, and the use of masks. The online classes were provided to the students and notes were shared through whatsApp in the form of PDF documents and Videos. Throughout the COVID-19 epidemic, Asha Deep Rehabilitation Center for Divyangjan demonstrated its dedication to the safety, well-being, and ongoing care of people with disabilities and their families.

During the COVID-19 epidemic, several institutions, including the Asha Deep Rehabilitation Center for Divyangjan, were confronted with considerable obstacles. The organization adopted a variety of preventative protocols in order to ensure the health and safety of children with special needs as well as the families that cared for them. These measurements consisted of the following:

1. Sanitizing Facilities The center made sure that its premises were sanitized on a regular basis to guarantee that

the children and the staff always worked in a clean and risk-free environment.

2. Handwashing: One of the most important parts of the center's plan to stop the spread of the virus was to encourage people to wash their hands often.

3. Wearing of Masks In order to lessen the possibility of infection spreading throughout the institution, the wearing of masks was strongly promoted.

4. The Center Provided Online Classes The center made it possible for students to continue their education by providing online classes. Students were given the opportunity to access educational materials while remaining in the comfort of their own homes thanks to this strategy.

5. The Center Adapted to the Digital Environment by distributing Notes over WhatsApp The center adapted to the digital environment by distributing instructional materials through WhatsApp in the form of PDF papers and videos. Students were able to continue their education at a distance thanks to this approach.

The Asha Deep Rehabilitation Center for Divyangjan shown an unflinching devotion to the safety, well-being, and continuous care of persons with disabilities and their families during the duration of the COVID-19 epidemic. These initiatives demonstrate the organization's dedication to pursuing its purpose despite the challenges that are now being faced.

Chapter 8
Future Undertakings

- Future undertakings of Asha Deep Rehabilitation Center for Divyangjan

Asha Deep Rehabilitation Center for Divyangjan will add class XII with Arts and Commerce courses in the future. Expanding educational opportunities will benefit students and parents. Taking Commerce and Arts will enable students to study economics, accounting, and business. This will gives pupils a good foundation for commerce-related careers. Extension to Class XII ensures continuity and stability for pupils.

At the Asha Deep Rehabilitation Center for Divyangjan, it is a move in the right direction to broaden educational options by introducing classes for students in their twelfth year of high school in the arts and commerce. This program will provide a number of advantages, not only to students but also to their parents, including the following:

1. Diverse Educational Options:

The availability of courses in both the arts and the business world gives students access to a wider variety of educational paths to pursue. They are given the opportunity to investigate topics such as economics, accounting, business, and the humanities, which are in line with their interests and goals for a future job.

2. A Solid Foundation for Careers Related to Commerce:

The Commerce concentration in particular provides students with fundamental information and abilities in the areas of accounting, finance, and business management. Those interested in pursuing jobs in sectors linked to commerce may find this foundation to be quite helpful.

3. Continuity in Education:

By extending the curriculum to Class XII, students will be able to finish their upper secondary education at the same institution in which they began it. This would provide continuity in education. Because of this continuity, children do not have to relocate to other schools after completing their tenth grade studies, which is a benefit for them.

4. Stability:

It is essential for kids who have special needs to have stability in their lives. These children have the opportunity to continue their education and grow as individuals within a secure and encouraging setting thanks to the fact that Asha Deep Rehabilitation Center offers classes up to the twelfth grade.

In a nutshell, the inclusion of Class XII at the center with courses in the arts and commerce broadens students' access to education, lays the groundwork for students' future professional endeavors, and fosters continuity and stability in the instruction of students who have unique educational requirements.

Conclusion

The following conclusion may be reached after analyzing the case study that was conducted on the Asha Deep Rehabilitation Center for Divyangjan:

The Asha Deep Rehabilitation Center for Divyangjan is a one-of-a-kind school that was founded with the intention of influencing society and shifting the perceptions of children who have special needs. It offers a balanced education that focuses on the development of academic, extracurricular, vocational, and life skills in addition to providing opportunities for these areas of development. The bulk of the rehabilitation center's clientele are Muslims and Hindus, and the facility has been successful in attracting pupils from a variety of regions located in the state of Bihar and keeping them as clients. The Asha Deep Rehabilitation Center is making an attempt to offer early intervention and rehabilitation in order to diagnose and correct hearing problems in children who have intellectual challenges and to provide these children with the chance to reach their full potential. In general, the Asha Deep Rehabilitation Center for Divyangjan is a model organization that makes major strides in enhancing the quality of life and education available to children in Bihar who have special needs.

The case study research on the special school provides insightful information on how inclusive education practices are applied and emphasizes the necessity of developing a welcoming and inclusive learning environment for all students. This information was gleaned from the investigation of a special school. The school's inclusive education strategy, which is focused on a student-centered approach, professional development for staff, collaboration with families and communities, and an inclusive culture, may serve as a model for other schools that seek to build their own inclusiveness strategy. This cooperation includes providing support and resources to families of students with special needs.

Appendixes

jftLVh lañ Mhñ ,yñ —(,u)04@0007@2003—16 REGISTERED NO. DL—(N)04/0007/2003—16

भारत का राजपत्र
The Gazette of India

vlk/kkj.k
EXTRAORDINARY
II[kk.M
PART II—Section 1
izkf/kdkj ls izdkf'kr
PUBLISHED BY AUTHORITY

lañ 59]ubZ fnYyh] cq/kokj] fnlEcj 28] 2016@ikS"k 07] 1938 ¼'kd½
No. 59]NEW DELHI, WEDNESDAY, DECEMBER 28, 2016/PAUSHA 07, 1938 (SAKA)

bl Hkkx esa fHkUu i`"B la[;k nh tkrh gS ftlls fd ;g vyx ladyu ds :i esa j[kk tk ldsA
Separate paging is given to this Part in order that it may be filed as a separate compilation.

MINISTRY OF LAW AND JUSTICE

(Legislative Department)

New Delhi, the th December, 282016/*Pausha* 17, 1938 (*Saka*)

The following Act of Parliament received the assent of the President on the 27th December, 2016, and is hereby published for general information:—

THE RIGHTS OF PERSONS WITH DISABILITIES ACT, 2016

(NO. 49 OF 2016)

[27*th December,* 2016]

An Act to give effect to the United Nations Convention on the Rights of Persons with Disabilities and for matters connected therewith or incidental thereto.

WHEREAS the United Nations General Assembly adopted its Convention on the Rights of Persons with Disabilities on the 13th day of December, 2006;

AND WHEREAS the aforesaid Convention lays down the following principles for empowerment of persons with disabilities,—

(*a*) respect for inherent dignity, individual autonomy including the freedom to make one's own choices, and independence of persons;

(*b*) non-discrimination;

(*c*) full and effective participation and inclusion in society;

(*d*) respect for difference and acceptance of persons with disabilities as part of human diversity and humanity;

(*e*) equality of opportunity;

(*f*)accessibility;

(*g*) equality between men and women;

(*h*) respect for the evolving capacities of children with disabilities and respect for the right of children with disabilities to preserve their identities;

AND WHEREAS India is a signatory to the said Convention;

AND WHEREAS India ratified the said Convention on the 1st day of October, 2007;

AND WHEREAS it is considered necessary to implement the Convention aforesaid.

BE it enacted by Parliament in the Sixty-seventh Year of the Republic of India as follows:—

CHAPTER I

PRELIMINARY

Short title and commencement.

1. (*1*) This Act may be called the Rights of Persons with Disabilities Act, 2016.

(2) It shall come into force on such date as the Central Government may, by notification in the Official Gazette, appoint.

Definitions.

2. In this Act, unless the context otherwise requires,—

(*a*) "appellate authority" means an authority notified under sub-section (*3*) of section 14 or sub-section (*1*) of section 53 or designated under sub-section (*1*) of section 59, as the case may be;

(*b*) "appropriate Government" means,—

(*i*) in relation to the Central Government or any establishment wholly or substantially financed by that Government, or a Cantonment Board constituted under the Cantonments Act, 2006, the Central Government;

(*ii*) in relation to a State Government or any establishment, wholly or substantially financed by that Government, or any local authority, other than a Cantonment Board, the State Government. 41 of 2006.

(*c*) "barrier" means any factor including communicational, cultural, economic, environmental, institutional, political, social, attitudinal or structural factors which hampers the full and effective participation of persons with disabilities in society;

(*d*) "care-giver" means any person including parents and other family Members who with or without payment provides care, support or assistance to a person with disability;

(*e*) "certifying authority" means an authority designated under sub-section (*1*) of section 57;

(*f*) "communication" includes means and formats of communication, languages, display of text, Braille, tactile communication, signs, large print, accessible multimedia, written, audio, video, visual displays, sign language, plain-language, human-reader, augmentative and alternative modes and accessible information and communication technology;

(*g*) "competent authority" means an authority appointed under section 49;

(*h*) "discrimination" in relation to disability, means any distinction, exclusion, restriction on the basis of disability which is the purpose or effect of impairing or nullifying the recognition, enjoyment or exercise on an equal basis with others of all human rights and fundamental freedoms in the political, economic, social, cultural, civil or any other field and includes all forms of discrimination and denial of reasonable accommodation;

(*i*) "establishment" includes a Government establishment and private establishment;

(*j*) "Fund" means the National Fund constituted under section 86;

(*k*) "Government establishment" means a corporation established by or under a Central Act or State Act or an authority or a body owned or controlled or aided by the Government or a local authority or a Government company as defined in section 2 of the Companies Act, 2013 and includes a Department of the Government;

18 of 2013.

(*l*) "high support" means an intensive support, physical, psychological and otherwise, which may be required by a person with benchmark disability for daily activities, to take independent and informed decision to access facilities and participating in all areas of life including education, employment, family and community life and treatment and therapy;

(*m*) "inclusive education" means a system of education wherein students with and without disability learn together and the system of teaching and learning is suitably adapted to meet the learning needs of different types of students with disabilities;

(*n*) "information and communication technology" includes all services and innovations relating to information and communication, including telecom services, web based services, electronic and print services, digital and virtual services;

(*o*) "institution" means an institution for the reception, care, protection, education, training, rehabilitation and any other activities for persons with disabilities;

(*p*) "local authority" means a Municipality or a Panchayat, as defined in clause(*e*) and clause (*f*) of article 243P of the Constitution; a Cantonment Board constituted under the Cantonments Act, 2006; and any other authority established under an Act of Parliament or a State Legislature to administer the civic affairs;

41 of 2006.

(*q*) "notification" means a notification published in the Official Gazette and the expression "notify" or "notified" shall be construed accordingly;

(*r*) "person with benchmark disability" means a person with not less than forty per cent. of a specified disability where specified disability has not been defined in measurable terms and includes a person with disability where specified disability has been defined in measurable terms, as certified by the certifying authority;

(*s*) "person with disability" means a person with long term physical, mental, intellectual or sensory impairment which, in interaction with barriers, hinders his full and effective participation in society equally with others;

(*t*) "person with disability having high support needs" means a person with benchmark disability certified under clause (*a*) of sub-section(2) of section 58 who needs high support;

(*u*) "prescribed" means prescribed by rules made under this Act;

(*v*) "private establishment" means a company, firm, cooperative or other society, associations, trust, agency, institution, organisation, union, factory or such other establishment as the appropriate Government may, by notification, specify;

(*w*) "public building" means a Government or private building, used or accessed by the public at large, including a building used for educational or vocational purposes, workplace, commercial activities, public utilities, religious, cultural, leisure or recreational activities, medical or health services, law enforcement agencies, reformatories or judicial foras, railway stations or platforms, roadways bus stands or terminus, airports or waterways;

(*x*) "public facilities and services" includes all forms of delivery of services to the public at large, including housing, educational and vocational trainings, employment and career advancement, shopping or marketing, religious, cultural, leisure or recreational, medical, health and rehabilitation, banking, finance and insurance, communication, postal and information, access to justice, public utilities, transportation;

(*y*) "reasonable accommodation" means necessary and appropriate modification and adjustments, without imposing a disproportionate or undue burden in a particular case, to ensure to persons with disabilities the enjoyment or exercise of rights equally with others;

(*z*) "registered organisation" means an association of persons with disabilities or a disabled person organisation, association of parents of persons with disabilities, association of persons with disabilities and family members, or a voluntary or non-governmental or charitable organisation or trust, society, or non-profit company working for the welfare of the persons with disabilities, duly registered under an Act of Parliament or a State Legislature;

(*za*) "rehabilitation" refers to a process aimed at enabling persons with disabilities to attain and maintain optimal, physical, sensory, intellectual, psychological environmental or social function levels;

(*zb*) "Special Employment Exchange" means any office or place established and maintained by the Government for the collection and furnishing of information, either by keeping of registers or otherwise, regarding—

(*i*) persons who seek to engage employees from amongst the persons with disabilities;

(*ii*) persons with benchmark disability who seek employment;

(*iii*) vacancies to which persons with benchmark disabilities seeking employment may be appointed;

(*zc*) "specified disability" means the disabilities as specified in the Schedule;

(*zd*) "transportation systems" includes road transport, rail transport, air transport, water transport, para transit systems for the last mile connectivity, road and street infrastructure, etc.;

(*ze*) "universal design" means the design of products, environments, programmes and services to be usable by all people to the greatest extent possible, without the need for adaptation or specialised design and shall apply to assistive devices including advanced technologies for particular group of persons with disabilities.

CHAPTER II

RIGHTS AND ENTITLEMENTS

Equality and non-discrimination.

3. (*1*) The appropriate Government shall ensure that the persons with disabilities enjoy the right to equality, life with dignity and respect for his or her integrity equally with others.

(*2*) The appropriate Government shall take steps to utilise the capacity of persons with disabilities by providing appropriate environment.

(*3*) No person with disability shall be discriminated on the ground of disability, unless it is shown that the impugned act or omission is a proportionate means of achieving a legitimate aim.

(*4*) No person shall be deprived of his or her personal liberty only on the ground of disability.

(*5*) The appropriate Government shall take necessary steps to ensure reasonable accommodation for persons with disabilities.

Women and children with disabilities.

4. (*1*) The appropriate Government and the local authorities shall take measures to ensure that the women and children with disabilities enjoy their rights equally with others.

(2) The appropriate Government and local authorities shall ensure that all children with disabilities shall have right on an equal basis to freely express their views on all matters affecting them and provide them appropriate support keeping in view their age and disability.".

Communit y life.

5. (*1*) The persons with disabilities shall have the right to live in the community.

(2) The appropriate Government shall endeavour that the persons with disabilities are,—

(*a*) not obliged to live in any particular living arrangement; and

(*b*) given access to a range of in-house, residential and other community support services, including personal assistance necessary to support living with due regard to age and gender.

Protection from cruelty and inhuman treatment.

6. (*1*) The appropriate Government shall take measures to protect persons with disabilities from being subjected to torture, cruel, inhuman or degrading treatment.

(2) No person with disability shall be a subject of any research without,—

(*i*) his or her free and informed consent obtained through accessible modes, means and formats of communication; and

(*ii*) prior permission of a Committee for Research on Disability constituted in the prescribed manner for the purpose by the appropriate Government in which not less than half of the Members shall themselves be either persons with disabilities or Members of the registered organisation as defined under clause (*z*) of section 2.

Protection from abuse, violence and exploitation.

7. (*1*) The appropriate Government shall take measures to protect persons with disabilities from all forms of abuse, violence and exploitation and to prevent the same, shall—

(*a*) take cognizance of incidents of abuse, violence and exploitation and provide legal remedies available against such incidents;

(*b*) take steps for avoiding such incidents and prescribe the procedure for its reporting;

(*c*) take steps to rescue, protect and rehabilitate victims of such incidents; and

(*d*) create awareness and make available information among the public.

(2) Any person or registered organisation who or which has reason to believe that an act of abuse, violence or exploitation has been, or is being, or is likely to be committed against any person with disability, may give information about it to the Executive Magistrate within the local limits of whose jurisdiction such incidents occur.

(*3*) The Executive Magistrate on receipt of such information, shall take immediate steps to stop or prevent its occurrence, as the case may be, or pass such order as he deems fit for the protection of such person with disability including an order—

(*a*) to rescue the victim of such act, authorising the police or any organisation working for persons with disabilities to provide for the safe custody or rehabilitation of such person, or both, as the case may be;

(*b*) for providing protective custody to the person with disability, if such person so desires;

(*c*) to provide maintenance to such person with disability.

(*4*) Any police officer who receives a complaint or otherwise comes to know of abuse, violence or exploitation towards any person with disability shall inform the aggrieved person of—

(*a*) his or her right to apply for protection under sub-section (*2*) and the particulars of the Executive Magistrate having jurisdiction to provide assistance;

(*b*) the particulars of the nearest organisation or institution working for the rehabilitation of persons with disabilities;

(*c*) the right to free legal aid; and

(*d*) the right to file a complaint under the provisions of this Act or any other law dealing with such offence:

Provided that nothing in this section shall be construed in any manner as to relieve the police officer from his duty to proceed in accordance with law upon receipt of information as to the commission of a cognizable offence.

(*5*) If the Executive Magistrate finds that the alleged act or behaviour constitutes an offence under the Indian Penal Code, or under any other law for the time being in force, he 45 of 1860.

may forward the complaint to that effect to the Judicial or Metropolitan Magistrate, as the case may be, having jurisdiction in the matter.

Protection and safety.

8. (*1*) The persons with disabilities shall have equal protection and safety in situations of risk, armed conflict, humanitarian emergencies and natural disasters.

(*2*) The National Disaster Management Authority and the State Disaster Management Authority shall take appropriate measures to ensure inclusion of persons with disabilities in its disaster management activities as defined under clause (*e*) of section 2 of the Disaster Management Act, 2005 for the safety and protection of persons with disabilities. 53 of 2005.

(*3*) The District Disaster Management Authority constituted under section 25 of the Disaster Management Act, 2005 shall maintain record of details of persons with disabilities in the district and take suitable measures to inform such persons of any situations of risk so 53 of 2005.

as

to enhance disaster preparedness.

(*4*) The authorities engaged in reconstruction activities subsequent to any situation of risk, armed conflict or natural disasters shall undertake such activities, in consultation with the concerned State Commissioner, in accordance with the accessibility requirements

of

persons with disabilities.

Home and family.

9. (*1*) No child with disability shall be separated from his or her parents on the ground of disability except on an order of competent court, if required, in the best interest of the child.

Reproductive rights.

(*2*) Where the parents are unable to take care of a child with disability, the competent court shall place such child with his or her near relations, and failing that within the community

in a family setting or in exceptional cases in shelter home run by the appropriate Government

Accessibility in voting.

or non-governmental organisation, as may be required.

10. (*1*) The appropriate Government shall ensure that persons with disabilities have access to appropriate information regarding reproductive and family planning.

Access to justice.

(*2*) No person with disability shall be subject to any medical procedure which leads to infertility without his or her free and informed consent.

11. The Election Commission of India and the State Election Commissions shall ensure that all polling stations are accessible to persons with disabilities and all materials related to the electoral process are easily understandable by and accessible to them.

12. (*1*) The appropriate Government shall ensure that persons with disabilities are able to exercise the right to access any court, tribunal, authority, commission or any other body having judicial or quasi-judicial or investigative powers without discrimination on the basis of disability.

(*2*) The appropriate Government shall take steps to put in place suitable support measures for persons with disabilities specially those living outside family and those disabled requiring high support for exercising legal rights.

(3) The National Legal Services Authority and the State Legal Services Authorities constituted under the Legal Services Authorities Act, 1987 shall make provisions including reasonable accommodation to ensure that persons with disabilities have access to any scheme, programme, facility or service offered by them equally with others. 39 of 1987.

(4) The appropriate Government shall take steps to—

(a) ensure that all their public documents are in accessible formats;

(b) ensure that the filing departments, registry or any other office of records are supplied with necessary equipment to enable filing, storing and referring to the documents and evidence in accessible formats; and

(c) make available all necessary facilities and equipment to facilitate recording of testimonies, arguments or opinion given by persons with disabilities in their preferred language and means of communication.

Legal capacity.

13. (1) The appropriate Government shall ensure that the persons with disabilities have right, equally with others, to own or inherit property, movable or immovable, control their financial affairs and have access to bank loans, mortgages and other forms of financial credit.

(2) The appropriate Government shall ensure that the persons with disabilities enjoy legal capacity on an equal basis with others in all aspects of life and have the right to equal recognition everywhere as any other person before the law.

(3) When a conflict of interest arises between a person providing support and a person with disability in a particular financial, property or other economic transaction, then such supporting person shall abstain from providing support to the person with disability in that transaction:

Provided that there shall not be a presumption of conflict of interest just on the basis that the supporting person is related to the person with disability by blood, affinity or adoption.

(4) A person with disability may alter, modify or dismantle any support arrangement and seek the support of another:

Provided that such alteration, modification or dismantling shall be prospective in nature and shall not nullify any third party transaction entered into by the person with disability with the aforesaid support arrangement.

(5) Any person providing support to the person with disability shall not exercise undue influence and shall respect his or her autonomy, dignity and privacy.

Provision for guardianship.

14. (1) Notwithstanding anything contained in any other law for the time being in force, on and from the date of commencement of this Act, where a district court or any designated authority, as notified by the State Government, finds that a person with disability, who had been provided adequate and appropriate support but is unable to take legally binding decisions, may be provided further support of a limited guardian to take legally binding decisions on his behalf in consultation with such person, in such manner, as may be prescribed by the State Government:

Provided that the District Court or the designated authority, as the case may be, may grant total support to the person with disability requiring such support or where the limited guardianship is to be granted repeatedly, in which case, the decision regarding the support to be provided shall be reviewed by the Court or the designated authority, as the case may be, to determine the nature and manner of support to be provided.

Explanation.—For the purposes of this sub-section, "limited guardianship" means a system of joint decision which operates on mutual understanding and trust between the guardian and the person with disability, which shall be limited to a specific period and for specific decision and situation and shall operate in accordance to the will of the person with disability.

(2) On and from the date of commencement of this Act, every guardian appointed under any provision of any other law for the time being in force, for a person with disability shall be deemed to function as a limited guardian.

(3) Any person with disability aggrieved by the decision of the designated authority appointing a legal guardian may prefer an appeal to such appellate authority, as may be notified by the State Government for the purpose.

Designation of authorities to support.

15. (1) The appropriate Government shall designate one or more authorities to mobilise the community and create social awareness to support persons with disabilities in exercise of their legal capacity.

(2) The authority designated under sub-section (1) shall take measures for setting up suitable support arrangements to exercise legal capacity by persons with disabilities living in institutions and those with high support needs and any other measures as may be required.

CHAPTER III

EDUCATION

Duty of educational institutions.

16. The appropriate Government and the local authorities shall endeavour that all educational institutions funded or recognised by them provide inclusive education to the children with disabilities and towards that end shall—

(*i*) admit them without discrimination and provide education and opportunities for sports and recreation activities equally with others;

(*ii*) make building, campus and various facilities accessible;

(*iii*) provide reasonable accommodation according to the individual's requirements;

(*iv*) provide necessary support individualised or otherwise in environments that maximise academic and social development consistent with the goal of full inclusion;

(*v*) ensure that the education to persons who are blind or deaf or both is imparted in the most appropriate languages and modes and means of communication;

(*vi*) detect specific learning disabilities in children at the earliest and take suitable pedagogical and other measures to overcome them;

(*vii*) monitor participation, progress in terms of attainment levels and completion of education in respect of every student with disability;

(*viii*) provide transportation facilities to the children with disabilities and also the attendant of the children with disabilities having high support needs.

Specific measures to promote and facilitate inclusive education.

17. The appropriate Government and the local authorities shall take the following measures for the purpose of section 16, namely:—

(*a*) to conduct survey of school going children in every five years for identifying children with disabilities, ascertaining their special needs and the extent to which these are being met:

Provided that the first survey shall be conducted within a period of two years from the date of commencement of this Act;

(*b*) to establish adequate number of teacher training institutions;

(*c*) to train and employ teachers, including teachers with disability who are qualified in sign language and Braille and also teachers who are trained in teaching children with intellectual disability;

(*d*) to train professionals and staff to support inclusive education at all levels of school education;

(*e*) to establish adequate number of resource centres to support educational institutions at all levels of school education;

(*f*) to promote the use of appropriate augmentative and alternative modes including means and formats of communication, Braille and sign language to supplement the use of one's own speech to fulfill the daily communication needs of persons with speech, communication or language disabilities and enables them to participate and contribute to their community and society;

(*g*) to provide books, other learning materials and appropriate assistive devices to students with benchmark disabilities free of cost up to the age of eighteen years;

(*h*) to provide scholarships in appropriate cases to students with benchmark disability;

(*i*) to make suitable modifications in the curriculum and examination system to meet the needs of students with disabilities such as extra time for completion of examination paper, facility of scribe or amanuensis, exemption from second and third language courses;

(*j*) to promote research to improve learning; and

(*k*) any other measures, as may be required.

18. The appropriate Government and the local authorities shall take measures to promote, protect and ensure participation of persons with disabilities in adult education and continuing education programmes equally with others. Adult education.

CHAPTER IV

SKILL DEVELOPMENT AND EMPLOYMENT

19. (*1*) The appropriate Government shall formulate schemes and programmes including provision of loans at concessional rates to facilitate and support employment of persons with disabilities especially for their vocational training and self-employment. Vocational training and self-employment.

(2) The schemes and programmes referred to in sub-section (*1*) shall provide for—

(*a*) inclusion of person with disability in all mainstream formal and non-formal vocational and skill training schemes and programmes;

(*b*) to ensure that a person with disability has adequate support and facilities to avail specific training;

(*c*) exclusive skill training programmes for persons with disabilities with active links with the market, for those with developmental, intellectual, multiple disabilities and autism;

(*d*) loans at concessional rates including that of microcredit;

(*e*) marketing the products made by persons with disabilities; and

(*f*) maintenance of disaggregated data on the progress made in the skill training and self-employment, including persons with disabilities.

20. (*1*) No Government establishment shall discriminate against any person with disability in any matter relating to employment: Non-discrimination in employment.

Provided that the appropriate Government may, having regard to the type of work carried on in any establishment, by notification and subject to such conditions, if any, exempt any establishment from the provisions of this section.

(2) Every Government establishment shall provide reasonable accommodation and appropriate barrier free and conducive environment to employees with disability.

(*3*) No promotion shall be denied to a person merely on the ground of disability.

(*4*) No Government establishment shall dispense with or reduce in rank, an employee who acquires a disability during his or her service:

Provided that, if an employee after acquiring disability is not suitable for the post he was holding, shall be shifted to some other post with the same pay scale and service benefits:

Provided further that if it is not possible to adjust the employee against any post, he may be kept on a supernumerary post until a suitable post is available or he attains the age of superannuation, whichever is earlier.

(*5*) The appropriate Government may frame policies for posting and transfer of employees with disabilities.

Equal opportunity policy.

21. (*1*) Every establishment shall notify equal opportunity policy detailing measures proposed to be taken by it in pursuance of the provisions of this Chapter in the manner as may be prescribed by the Central Government.

(*2*) Every establishment shall register a copy of the said policy with the Chief Commissioner or the State Commissioner, as the case may be.

Maintenance of records.

22. (*1*) Every establishment shall maintain records of the persons with disabilities in relation to the matter of employment, facilities provided and other necessary information in compliance with the provisions of this Chapter in such form and manner as may be prescribed by the Central Government.

(*2*) Every employment exchange shall maintain records of persons with disabilities seeking employment.

(*3*) The records maintained under sub-section (*1*) shall be open to inspection at all reasonable hours by such persons as may be authorised in their behalf by the appropriate Government.

Appointment of Grievance Redressal Officer.

23. (*1*) Every Government establishment shall appoint a Grievance Redressal Officer for the purpose of section 19 and shall inform the Chief Commissioner or the State Commissioner, as the case may be, about the appointment of such officer.

(*2*) Any person aggrieved with the non-compliance of the provisions of section 20, may file a complaint with the Grievance Redressal Officer, who shall investigate it and shall take up the matter with the establishment for corrective action.

(*3*) The Grievance Redressal Officer shall maintain a register of complaints in the manner as may be prescribed by the Central Government, and every complaint shall be inquired within two weeks of its registration.

(*4*) If the aggrieved person is not satisfied with the action taken on his or her complaint, he or she may approach the District-Level Committee on disability.

CHAPTER V

SOCIAL SECURITY, HEALTH, REHABILITATION AND RECREATION

Social security.

24. (*1*) The appropriate Government shall within the limit of its economic capacity and development formulate necessary schemes and programmes to safeguard and promote the right of persons with disabilities for adequate standard of living to enable them to live independently or in the community:

Provided that the quantum of assistance to the persons with disabilities under such schemes and programmes shall be at least twenty-five per cent. higher than the similar schemes applicable to others.

(*2*) The appropriate Government while devising these schemes and programmes shall give due consideration to the diversity of disability, gender, age, and socio-economic status.

(*3*) The schemes under sub-section (*1*) shall provide for,—

(*a*) community centres with good living conditions in terms of safety, sanitation, health care and counselling;

(*b*) facilities for persons including children with disabilities who have no family or have been abandoned, or are without shelter or livelihood;

(*c*) support during natural or man-made disasters and in areas of conflict;

(*d*) support to women with disability for livelihood and for upbringing of their children;

(*e*) access to safe drinking water and appropriate and accessible sanitation facilities especially in urban slums and rural areas;

(*f*) provisions of aids and appliances, medicine and diagnostic services and corrective surgery free of cost to persons with disabilities with such income ceiling as may be notified;

(*g*) disability pension to persons with disabilities subject to such income ceiling as may be notified;

(*h*) unemployment allowance to persons with disabilities registered with Special Employment Exchange for more than two years and who could not be placed in any gainful occupation;

(*i*) care-giver allowance to persons with disabilities with high support needs;

(*j*) comprehensive insurance scheme for persons with disability, not covered under the Employees State Insurance Schemes, or any other statutory or Government-sponsored insurance schemes;

(*k*) any other matter which the appropriate Government may think fit.

25. (*1*) The appropriate Government and the local authorities shall take necessary measures for the persons with disabilities to provide,— Healthcare.

(*a*) free healthcare in the vicinity specially in rural area subject to such family income as may be notified;

(*b*) barrier-free access in all parts of Government and private hospitals and other healthcare institutions and centres;

(*c*) priority in attendance and treatment.

(2) The appropriate Government and the local authorities shall take measures and make schemes or programmes to promote healthcare and prevent the occurrence of disabilities and for the said purpose shall—

(*a*) undertake or cause to be undertaken surveys, investigations and research concerning the cause of occurrence of disabilities;

(*b*) promote various methods for preventing disabilities;

(*c*) screen all the children at least once in a year for the purpose of identifying "at-risk" cases;

(*d*) provide facilities for training to the staff at the primary health centres;

(*e*) sponsor or cause to be sponsored awareness campaigns and disseminate or cause to be disseminated information for general hygiene, health and sanitation;

(*f*) take measures for pre-natal, perinatal and post-natal care of mother and child;

(*g*) educate the public through the pre-schools, schools, primary health centres, village level workers and *anganwadi* workers;

(*h*) create awareness amongst the masses through television, radio and other mass media on the causes of disabilities and the preventive measures to be adopted;

(*i*) healthcare during the time of natural disasters and other situations of risk;

(*j*) essential medical facilities for life saving emergency treatment and procedures; and

(*k*) sexual and reproductive healthcare especially for women with disability.

26. The appropriate Government shall, by notification, make insurance schemes for their employees with disabilities. Insurance schemes.

27. (*1*) The appropriate Government and the local authorities shall within their economic capacity and development, undertake or cause to be undertaken services and programmes of Rehabilitation.

rehabilitation, particularly in the areas of health, education and employment for all persons with disabilities.

(2) For the purposes of sub-section (1), the appropriate Government and the local authorities may grant financial assistance to non-Governmental Organisations.

(3) The appropriate Government and the local authorities, while formulating rehabilitation policies shall consult the non-Governmental Organisations working for the cause of persons with disabilities.

Research and development.

28. The appropriate Government shall initiate or cause to be initiated research and development through individuals and institutions on issues which shall enhance habilitatio and rehabilitation and on such other issues which are necessary for the empowerment of persons with disabilities.

Culture and recreation.

29. The appropriate Government and the local authorities shall take measures to promote and protect the rights of all persons with disabilities to have a cultural life and to participate in recreational activities equally with others which include,—

(*a*) facilities, support and sponsorships to artists and writers with disability to pursue their interests and talents;

(*b*) establishment of a disability history museum which chronicles and interprets the historical experiences of persons with disabilities;

(*c*) making art accessible to persons with disabilities;

(*d*) promoting recreation centres, and other associational activities;

(*e*) facilitating participation in scouting, dancing, art classes, outdoor camps and adventure activities;

(*f*) redesigning courses in cultural and arts subjects to enable participation and access for persons with disabilities;

(*g*) developing technology, assistive devices and equipments to facilitate access and inclusion for persons with disabilities in recreational activities; and

(*h*) ensuring that persons with hearing impairment can have access to television programmes with sign language interpretation or sub-titles.

Sporting activities.

30. (1) The appropriate Government shall take measures to ensure effective participation in sporting activities of the persons with disabilities.

(2) The sports authorities shall accord due recognition to the right of persons with disabilities to participate in sports and shall make due provisions for the inclusion of persons with disabilities in their schemes and programmes for the promotion and development of sporting talents.

(3) Without prejudice to the provisions contained in sub-sections (1) and (2), the appropriate Government and the sports authorities shall take measures to,—

(*a*) restructure courses and programmes to ensure access, inclusion and participation of persons with disabilities in all sporting activities;

(*b*) redesign and support infrastructure facilities of all sporting activities for persons with disabilities;

(*c*) develop technology to enhance potential, talent, capacity and ability in sporting activities of all persons with disabilities;

(*d*) provide multi-sensory essentials and features in all sporting activities to ensure effective participation of all persons with disabilities;

(*e*) allocate funds for development of state of art sport facilities for training of persons with disabilities;

(*f*) promote and organise disability specific sporting events for persons with disabilities and also facilitate awards to the winners and other participants of such sporting events.

CHAPTER VI

SPECIAL PROVISIONS FOR PERSONS WITH BENCHMARK DISABIILITES

31. (*1*) Notwithstanding anything contained in the Rights of Children to Free and Compulsory Education Act, 2009, every child with benchmark disability between the age of six to eighteen years shall have the right to free education in a neighbourhood school, or in a special school, of his choice. Free education for children with benchmark disabilities.

'09.

(*2*) The appropriate Government and local authorities shall ensure that every child with benchmark disability has access to free education in an appropriate environment till he attains the age of eighteen years.

32. (*1*) All Government institutions of higher education and other higher education institutions receiving aid from the Government shall reserve not less than five per cent. seats for persons with benchmark disabilities. Reservation in higher educational institutions.

(*2*) The persons with benchmark disabilities shall be given an upper age relaxation of five years for admission in institutions of higher education.

33. The appropriate Government shall— Identification of posts for reservation.

(*i*) identify posts in the establishments which can be held by respective category of persons with benchmark disabilities in respect of the vacancies reserved in accordance with the provisions of section 34;

(*ii*) constitute an expert committee with representation of persons with benchmark disabilities for identification of such posts; and

(*iii*) undertake periodic review of the identified posts at an interval not exceeding three years.

34. (*1*) Every appropriate Government shall appoint in every Government establishment, not less than four per cent. of the total number of vacancies in the cadre strength in each group of posts meant to be filled with persons with benchmark disabilities of which, one per cent. each shall be reserved for persons with benchmark disabilities under clauses (*a*), (*b*) and (*c*) and one per cent. for persons with benchmark disabilities under clauses (*d*) and (*e*), namely:— Reservation.

(*a*) blindness and low vision;

(*b*) deaf and hard of hearing;

(*c*) locomotor disability including cerebral palsy, leprosy cured, dwarfism, acid attack victims and muscular dystrophy;

(*d*) autism, intellectual disability, specific learning disability and mental illness;

(*e*) multiple disabilities from amongst persons under clauses (*a*) to (*d*) including deaf-blindness in the posts identified for each disabilities:

Provided that the reservation in promotion shall be in accordance with such instructions as are issued by the appropriate Government from time to time:

Provided further that the appropriate Government, in consultation with the Chief Commissioner or the State Commissioner, as the case may be, may, having regard to the type of work carried out in any Government establishment, by notification and subject to such conditions, if any, as may be specified in such notifications exempt any Government establishment from the provisions of this section.

(*2*) Where in any recruitment year any vacancy cannot be filled up due to non-availability of a suitable person with benchmark disability or for any other sufficient reasons, such vacancy shall be carried forward in the succeeding recruitment year and if in the succeeding recruitment year also suitable person with benchmark disability is not available, it may first be filled by interchange among the five categories and only when there is no person with disability available for the post in that year, the employer shall fill up the vacancy by appointment of a person, other than a person with disability:

Provided that if the nature of vacancies in an establishment is such that a given category of person cannot be employed, the vacancies may be interchanged among the five categories with the prior approval of the appropriate Government.

(*3*) The appropriate Government may, by notification, provide for such relaxation of upper age limit for employment of persons with benchmark disability, as it thinks fit.

Incentives to employers in private sector.

35. The appropriate Government and the local authorities shall, within the limit of their economic capacity and development, provide incentives to employer in private sector to ensure that at least five per cent. of their work force is composed of persons with benchmark disability.

Special employment exchange.

36. The appropriate Government may, by notification, require that from such date, the employer in every establishment shall furnish such information or return as may be prescribed by the Central Government in relation to vacancies appointed for persons with benchmark disability that have occurred or are about to occur in that establishment to such special employment exchange as may be notified by the Central Government and the establishment shall thereupon comply with such requisition.

Special schemes and development programmes.

37. The appropriate Government and the local authorities shall, by notification, make schemes in favour of persons with benchmark disabilities, to provide,—

(*a*) five per cent. reservation in allotment of agricultural land and housing in all relevant schemes and development programmes, with appropriate priority to women with benchmark disabilities;

(*b*) five per cent. reservation in all poverty alleviation and various developmental schemes with priority to women with benchmark disabilities;

(*c*) five per cent. reservation in allotment of land on concessional rate, where such land is to be used for the purpose of promoting housing, shelter, setting up of occupation, business, enterprise, recreation centres and production centres.

CHAPTER VII

SPECIAL PROVISIONS FOR PERSONS WITH DISABILITIES WITH HIGH SUPPORT NEEDS

Special provisions for persons with disabilities with high support.

38. (*1*) Any person with benchmark disability, who considers himself to be in need of high support, or any person or organisation on his or her behalf, may apply to an authority, to be notified by the appropriate Government, requesting to provide high support.

(*2*) On receipt of an application under sub-section (*1*), the authority shall refer it to an Assessment Board consisting of such Members as may be prescribed by the Central Government.

(*3*) The Assessment Board shall assess the case referred to it under sub-section (*1*) in such manner as may be prescribed by the Central Government, and shall send a report to the authority certifying the need of high support and its nature.

(*4*) On receipt of a report under sub-section (*3*), the authority shall take steps to provide support in accordance with the report and subject to relevant schemes and orders of the appropriate Government in this behalf.

CHAPTER VIII

DUTIES AND RESPONSIBILITIES OF APPROPRIATE GOVERNMENTS

Awareness campaigns.

39. (*1*) The appropriate Government, in consultation with the Chief Commissioner or the State Commissioner, as the case may be, shall conduct, encourage, support or promote awareness campaigns and sensitisation programmes to ensure that the rights of the persons with disabilities provided under this Act are protected.

(*2*) The programmes and campaigns specified under sub-section (*1*) shall also,—

(*a*) promote values of inclusion, tolerance, empathy and respect for diversity;

(*b*) advance recognition of the skills, merits and abilities of persons with disabilities and of their contributions to the workforce, labour market and professional fee;

(*c*) foster respect for the decisions made by persons with disabilities on all matters related to family life, relationships, bearing and raising children;

(*d*) provide orientation and sensitisation at the school, college, University and professional training level on the human condition of disability and the rights of persons with disabilities;

(*e*) provide orientation and sensitisation on disabling conditions and rights of persons with disabilities to employers, administrators and co-workers;

(*f*) ensure that the rights of persons with disabilities are included in the curriculum in Universities, colleges and schools.

40. The Central Government shall, in consultation with the Chief Commissioner, formulate rules for persons with disabilities laying down the standards of accessibility for the physical environment, transportation, information and communications, including appropriate technologies and systems, and other facilities and services provided to the public in urban and rural areas. Accessibility.

41. (*1*) The appropriate Government shall take suitable measures to provide,— Access to transport.

(*a*) facilities for persons with disabilities at bus stops, railway stations and airports conforming to the accessibility standards relating to parking spaces, toilets, ticketing counters and ticketing machines;

(*b*) access to all modes of transport that conform the design standards, including retrofitting old modes of transport, wherever technically feasible and safe for persons with disabilities, economically viable and without entailing major structural changes in design;

(*c*) accessible roads to address mobility necessary for persons with disabilities.

(2) The appropriate Government shall develop schemes programmes to promote the personal mobility of persons with disabilities at affordable cost to provide for,—

(*a*) incentives and concessions;

(*b*) retrofitting of vehicles; and

(*c*) personal mobility assistance.

42. The appropriate Government shall take measures to ensure that,— Access to information and communication technology.

(*i*) all contents available in audio, print and electronic media are in accessible format;

(*ii*) persons with disabilities have access to electronic media by providing audio description, sign language interpretation and close captioning;

(*iii*) electronic goods and equipment which are meant for every day use are available in universal design.

43. The appropriate Government shall take measures to promote development, production and distribution of universally designed consumer products and accessories for general use for persons with disabilities. Consumer goods.

44. (*1*) No establishment shall be granted permission to build any structure if the building plan does not adhere to the rules formulated by the Central Government under section 40. Mandatory observance of accessibility norms.

(2) No establishment shall be issued a certificate of completion or allowed to take occupation of a building unless it has adhered to the rules formulated by the Central Government.

45. (*1*) All existing public buildings shall be made accessible in accordance with the rules formulated by the Central Government within a period not exceeding five years from the date of notification of such rules: Time limit for making existing infrastructure and premises accessible and action for that purpose.

Provided that the Central Government may grant extension of time to the States on a case to case basis for adherence to this provision depending on their state of preparedness and other related parameters.

(2) The appropriate Government and the local authorities shall formulate and publish an action plan based on prioritisation, for providing accessibility in all their buildings and spaces providing essential services such as all primary health centres, civil hospitals, schools, railway stations and bus stops.

Time limit for accessibility by service providers.

46. The service providers whether Government or private shall provide services in accordance with the rules on accessibility formulated by the Central Government under section 40 within a period of two years from the date of notification of such rules:

Provided that the Central Government in consultation with the Chief Commissioner may grant extension of time for providing certain category of services in accordance with the said rules.

Human resource development.

47. (*1*) Without prejudice to any function and power of Rehabilitation Council of India constituted under the Rehabilitation Council of India Act, 1992, the appropriate Government shall endeavour to develop human resource for the purposes of this Act and to that end shall,— 34 of 1992.

(*a*) mandate training on disability rights in all courses for the training of Panchayati Raj Members, legislators, administrators, police officials, judges and lawyers;

(*b*) induct disability as a component for all education courses for schools, colleges and University teachers, doctors, nurses, para-medical personnel, social welfare officers, rural development officers, asha workers, *anganwadi* workers, engineers, architects, other professionals and community workers;

(*c*) initiate capacity building programmes including training in independent living and community relationships for families, members of community and other stakeholders and care providers on care giving and support;

(*d*) ensure independence training for persons with disabilities to build community relationships on mutual contribution and respect;

(*e*) conduct training programmes for sports teachers with focus on sports, games, adventure activities;

(*f*) any other capacity development measures as may be required.

(2) All Universities shall promote teaching and research in disability studies including establishment of study centres for such studies.

(*3*) In order to fulfil the obligation stated in sub-section (*1*), the appropriate Government shall in every five years undertake a need based analysis and formulate plans for the recruitment, induction, sensitisation, orientation and training of suitable personnel to undertake the various responsibilities under this Act.

Social audit.

48. The appropriate Government shall undertake social audit of all general schemes and programmes involving the persons with disabilities to ensure that the scheme and programmes do not have an adverse impact upon the persons with disabilities and need the requirements and concerns of persons with disabilities.

CHAPTER IX

REGISTRATION OF INSTITUTIONS FOR PERSONS WITH DISABILITIES AND GRANTS TO SUCH INSTITUTIONS

Competent authority.

49. The State Government shall appoint an authority as it deems fit to be a competent authority for the purposes of this Chapter.

Registration.

50. Save as otherwise provided under this Act, no person shall establish or maintain any institution for persons with disabilities except in accordance with a certificate of registration issued in this behalf by the competent authority:

Provided that an institution for care of mentally ill persons, which holds a valid licence under section 8 of the Mental Health Act, 1987 or any other Act for the time being in force, shall not be required to be registered under this Act. 14 of 1987.

51. (*1*) Every application for a certificate of registration shall be made to the competent authority in such form and in such manner as may be prescribed by the State Government.

Application and grant of certificate of registration.

(2) On receipt of an application under sub-section (*1*), the competent authority shall make such enquiries as it may deem fit and on being satisfied that the applicant has complied with the requirements of this Act and the rules made thereunder, it shall grant a certificate of registration to the applicant within a period of ninety days of receipt of application and if not satisfied, the competent authority shall, by order, refuse to grant the certificate applied for:

Provided that before making any order refusing to grant a certificate, the competent authority shall give the applicant a reasonable opportunity of being heard and every order of refusal to grant a certificate shall be communicated to the applicant in writing.

(*3*) No certificate of registration shall be granted under sub-section (2) unless the institution with respect to which an application has been made is in a position to provide such facilities and meet such standards as may be prescribed by the State Government.

(*4*) The certificate of registration granted under sub-section (2) ,—

(*a*) shall, unless revoked under section 52 remain in force for such period as may be prescribed by the State Government;

(*b*) may be renewed from time to time for a like period; and

(*c*) shall be in such form and shall be subject to such conditions as may be prescribed by the State Government.

(*5*) An application for renewal of a certificate of registration shall be made not less than sixty days before the expiry of the period of validity.

(*6*) A copy of the certificate of registration shall be displayed by the institution in a conspicuous place.

(*7*) Every application made under sub-section (*1*) or sub-section (*5*) shall be disposed of by the competent authority within such period as may be prescribed by the State Government.

52. (*1*) The competent authority may, if it has reason to believe that the holder of a certificate of registration granted under sub-section (2) of section 51 has,—

Revocation of registration.

(*a*) made a statement in relation to any application for the issue or renewal of the certificate which is incorrect or false in material particulars; or

(*b*) committed or has caused to be committed any breach of rules or any conditions subject to which the certificate was granted,

it may, after making such inquiry, as it deems fit, by order, revoke the certificate:

Provided that no such order shall be made until an opportunity is given to the holder of the certificate to show cause as to why the certificate of registration shall not be revoked.

(2) Where a certificate of registration in respect of an institution has been revoked under sub-section (*1*), such institution shall cease to function from the date of such revocation:

Provided that where an appeal lies under section 53 against the order of revocation, such institution shall cease to function,—

(*a*) where no appeal has been preferred immediately on the expiry of the period prescribed for the filing of such appeal; or

(*b*) where such appeal has been preferred, but the order of revocation has been upheld, from the date of the order of appeal.

(*3*) On the revocation of a certificate of registration in respect of an institution, the competent authority may direct that any person with disability who is an inmate of such institution on the date of such revocation, shall be—

(*a*) restored to the custody of his or her parent, spouse or lawful guardian, as the case may be; or (*b*) transferred to any other institution specified by the competent authority.

(*4*) Every institution which holds a certificate of registration which is revoked under this section shall, immediately after such revocation, surrender such certificate to the competent authority.

Appeal.

53. (*1*) Any person aggrieved by the order of the competent authority refusing to grant a certificate of registration or revoking a certificate of registration may, within such period as may be prescribed by the State Government, prefer an appeal to such appellate authority, as may be notified by the State Government against such refusal or revocation.

(2) The order of the appellate authority on such appeal shall be final.

Act not to apply to institutions established or maintained by Central or State Government.

54. Nothing contained in this Chapter shall apply to an institution for persons with disabilities established or maintained by the Central Government or a State Government.

Assistance to registered institutions.

55. The appropriate Government may within the limits of their economic capacity and development, grant financial assistance to registered institutions to provide services and to implement the schemes and programmes in pursuance of the provisions of this Act.

CHAPTER X

CERTIFICATION OF SPECIFIED DISABILITIES

Guidelines for assessment of specified disabilities.

56. The Central Government shall notify guidelines for the purpose of assessing the extent of specified disability in a person.

Designation of certifying authorities.

57. (*1*) The appropriate Government shall designate persons, having requisite qualifications and experience, as certifying authorities, who shall be competent to issue the certificate of disability.

(*2*) The appropriate Government shall also notify the jurisdiction within which and the terms and conditions subject to which, the certifying authority shall perform its certification functions.

Procedure for certification.

58. (*1*) Any person with specified disability, may apply, in such manner as may be prescribed by the Central Government, to a certifying authority having jurisdiction, for issuing of a certificate of disability.

(2) On receipt of an application under sub-section (*1*), the certifying authority shall assess the disability of the concerned person in accordance with relevant guidelines notified under section 56, and shall, after such assessment, as the case may be,—

(*a*) issue a certificate of disability to such person, in such form as may be prescribed by the Central Government;

(*b*) inform him in writing that he has no specified disability.

(*3*) The certificate of disability issued under this section shall be valid across the country.

Appeal against a decision of certifying authority.

59. (*1*) Any person aggrieved with decision of the certifying authority, may appeal against such decision, within such time and in such manner as may be prescribed by the State Government, to such appellate authority as the State Government may designate for the purpose.

(2) On receipt of an appeal, the appellate authority shall decide the appeal in such manner as may be prescribed by the State Government.

CHAPTER XI

CENTRAL AND STATE ADVISORY BOARDS ON DISABILITY AND DISTRICT LEVEL COMMITTEE

Constitution of Central Advisory Board on Disability.

60. *(1)* The Central Government shall, by notification, constitute a body to be known as the Central Advisory Board on Disability to exercise the powers conferred on, and to perform the functions assigned to it, under this Act.

(2) The Central Advisory Board shall consist of,—

(*a*) the Minister in charge of Department of Disability Affairs in the Central Government, Chairperson, *ex officio*;

(*b*) the Minister of State in charge dealing with Department of Disability Affairs in the Ministry in the Central Government, Vice Chairperson, *ex officio*;

(*c*) three Members of Parliament, of whom two shall be elected by Lok Sabha and one by the Rajya Sabha, Members, *ex officio*;

(*d*) the Ministers in charge of Disability Affairs of all States and Administrators or Lieutenant Governors of the Union territories, Members, *ex officio*;

(*e*) Secretaries to the Government of India in charge of the Ministries or Departments of Disability Affairs, Social Justice and Empowerment, School Education and Literacy, and Higher Education, Women and Child Development, Expenditure, Personnel and Training, Administrative Reforms and Public Grievances, Health and Family Welfare, Rural Development, Panchayati Raj, Industrial Policy and Promotion, Urban Development, Housing and Urban Poverty Alleviation, Science and Technology, Communications and Information Technology, Legal Affairs, Public Enterprises, Youth Affairs and Sports, Road Transport and Highways and Civil Aviation, Members, *ex officio*;

(*f*) Secretary, National Institute of Transforming India (NITI) Aayog, Member, *ex officio;*

(*g*) Chairperson, Rehabilitation Council of India, Member, *ex officio*;

(*h*) Chairperson, National Trust for the Welfare of Persons with Autism, Cerebral Palsy, Mental Retardation and Multiple Disabilities, Member, *ex officio*;

(*i*) Chairman-cum-Managing Director, National Handicapped Finance Development Corporation, Member, *ex officio*;

(*j*) Chairman-cum-Managing Director, Artificial Limbs Manufacturing Corporation, Member, *ex officio;*

(*k*) Chairman, Railway Board, Member, *ex officio*;

(*l*) Director-General, Employment and Training, Ministry of Labour and Employment, Member, *ex officio*;

(*m*) Director, National Council for Educational Research and Training, Member, *ex officio*;

(*n*) Chairperson, National Council of Teacher Education, Member, *ex officio*;

(*o*) Chairperson, University Grants Commission, Member, *ex officio*;

(*p*) Chairperson, Medical Council of India, Member, *ex officio*;

(*q*) Directors of the following Institutes:—

(*i*) National Institute for the Visually Handicapped, Dehradun;

(*ii*) National Institute for the Mentally Handicapped, Secundrabad;

(*iii*) Pandit Deen Dayal Upadhyay Institute for the Physically Handicapped, New Delhi;

(*iv*) Ali Yavar Jung National Institute for the Hearing Handicapped, Mumbai;

(*v*) National Institute for the Orthopaedically Handicapped, Kolkata;

(*vi*) National Institute of Rehabilitation Training and Research, Cuttack;

(*vii*) National Institute for Empowerment of Persons with Multiple Disabilities, Chennai;

(*viii*) National Institute for Mental Health and Sciences, Bangalore;

(*ix*) Indian Sign Language Research and Training Centre, New Delhi, Members, *ex officio;*

(*r*) Members to be nominated by the Central Government,—

(*i*) five Members who are experts in the field of disability and rehabilitation;

(*ii*) ten Members, as far as practicable, being persons with disabilities, to represent non-Governmental Organisations concerned with disabilities or disabled persons organisations:

Provided that out of the ten Members nominated, at least, five Members shall be women and at least one person each shall be from the Scheduled Castes and the Scheduled Tribes;

(*iii*) up to three representatives of national level chambers of commerce and industry;

(*s*) Joint Secretary to the Government of India dealing with the subject of disability policy, Member-Secretary, *ex officio*.

Terms and conditions of Service of members.

61. (*1*) Save as otherwise provided under this Act, a Member of the Central Advisory Board nominated under clause (*r*) of sub-section (*2*) of section 60 shall hold office for a term of three years from the date of his nomination:

Provided that such a Member shall, notwithstanding the expiration of his term, continue to hold office until his successor enters upon his office.

(*2*) The Central Government may, if it thinks fit, remove any Member nominated under clause (*r*) of sub-section (*2*) of section 60, before the expiry of his term of office after giving him a reasonable opportunity of showing cause against the same.

(*3*)A Member nominated under clause (*r*) of sub-section (*2*) of section 60 may at any time resign his office by writing under his hand addressed to the Central Government and the seat of the said Member shall thereupon becomes vacant.

(*4*) A casual vacancy in the Central Advisory Board shall be filled by a fresh nomination and the person nominated to fill the vacancy shall hold office only for the remainder of the term for which the Member in whose place he was so nominated.

(*5*) A Member nominated under sub-clause (*i*) or sub-clause (*iii*) of clause (*r*) of sub-section (*2*) of section 60 shall be eligible for renomination.

(*6*) The Members nominated under sub-clause (*i*) and sub-clause (*ii*) of clause (*r*) of sub-section (*2*) of section 60 shall receive such allowances as may be prescribed by the Central Government.

Disqualifications.

62. (*1*) No person shall be a Member of the Central Advisory Board, who —

(*a*) is, or at any time has been, adjudged insolvent or has suspended payment of his debts or has compounded with his creditors, or

(*b*) is of unsound mind and stands so declared by a competent court, or

(*c*) is, or has been, convicted of an offence which, in the opinion of the Central Government, involves moral turpitude, or

(*d*) is, or at any time has been, convicted of an offence under this Act, or

(*e*) has so abused his position in the opinion of the Central Government as a Member so as to render his continuance in the office is prejudicial interests of the general public.

(*2*) No order of removal shall be made by the Central Government under this section unless the Member concerned has been given a reasonable opportunity of showing cause against the same.

(3) Notwithstanding anything contained in sub-section (1) or sub-section (5) of section 61, a Member who has been removed under this section shall not be eligible for renomination as a Member.

63. If a Member of the Central Advisory Board becomes subject to any of the disqualifications specified in section 62, his seat shall become vacant. Vacation of seats by Members.

64. The Central Advisory Board shall meet at least once in every six months and shall observe such rules of procedure in regard to the transaction of business at its meetings as may be prescribed. Meetings of the Central Advisory Board on disability.

65. (1) Subject to the provisions of this Act, the Central Advisory Board on disability shall be the national-level consultative and advisory body on disability matters, and shall facilitate the continuous evolution of a comprehensive policy for the empowerment of persons with disabilities and the full enjoyment of rights. Functions of Central Advisory Board on disability.

(2) In particular and without prejudice to the generality of the foregoing provisions, the Central Advisory Board on disability shall perform the following functions, namely:

(a) advise the Central Government and the State Governments on policies, programmes, legislation and projects with respect to disability;

(b) develop a national policy to address issues concerning persons with disabilities;

(c) review and coordinate the activities of all Departments of the Government and other Governmental and non-Governmental Organisations which are dealing with matters relating to persons with disabilities;

(d) take up the cause of persons with disabilities with the concerned authorities and the international organisations with a view to provide for schemes and projects for the persons with disabilities in the national plans;

(e) recommend steps to ensure accessibility, reasonable accommodation, non-discrimination for persons with disabilities *vis-à-vis* information, services and the built environment and their participation in social life;

(f) monitor and evaluate the impact of laws, policies and programmes to achieve full participation of persons with disabilities; and

(g) such other functions as may be assigned from time to time by the Central Government.

66. (1) Every State Government shall, by notification, constitute a body to be known as the State Advisory Board on disability to exercise the powers conferred on, and to perform the function assigned to it, under this Act. State Advisory Board on disability.

(2) The State Advisory Board shall consist of—

(a) the Minister in charge of the Department in the State Government dealing with disability matters, Chairperson, *ex officio*;

(b) the Minister of State or the Deputy Minister in charge of the Department in the State Government dealing with disability matters, if any, Vice-Chairperson, *ex officio*;

(c) secretaries to the State Government in charge of the Departments of Disability Affairs, School Education, Literacy and Higher Education, Women and Child Development, Finance, Personnel and Training, Health and Family Welfare, Rural Development, Panchayati Raj, Industrial Policy and Promotion, Labour and Employment, Urban Development, Housing and Urban Poverty Alleviation, Science and Technology, Information Technology, Public Enterprises, Youth Affairs and Sports, Road Transport and any other Department, which the State Government considers necessary, Members, *ex officio*;

(d) three Members of the State Legislature of whom two shall be elected by the Legislative Assembly and one by the Legislative Council, if any, and where there is no Legislative Council, three Members shall be elected by the Legislative Assembly, Members, *ex officio*;

(*e*) Members to be nominated by the State Government:—

(*i*) five Members who are experts in the field of disability and rehabilitation;

(*ii*) five Members to be nominated by the State Government by rotation to represent the districts in such manner as may be prescribed:

Provided that no nomination under this sub-clause shall be made except on the recommendation of the district administration concerned;

(*iii*) ten persons as far as practicable, being persons with disabilities, to represent non-Governmental Organisations or associations which are concerned with disabilities:

Provided that out of the ten persons nominated under this clause, at least, five shall be women and at least one person each shall be from the Scheduled Castes and the Scheduled Tribes;

(*iv*) not more than three representatives of the State Chamber of Commerce and Industry;

(*f*) officer not below the rank of Joint Secretary in the Department dealing with disability matters in the State Government, Member-Secretary, *ex officio*.

Terms and conditions of service of Members.

67. (*1*) Save as otherwise provided under this Act, a Member of the State Advisory Board nominated under clause (*e*) of sub-section (2) of section 66, shall hold office for a term of three years from the date of his nomination:

Provided that such a Member shall, notwithstanding the expiration of his term, continue to hold office until his successor enters upon his office.

(*2*) The State Government may, if it thinks fit, remove any Member nominated under clause (*e*) of sub-section (2) of section 66, before the expiry of his term of office after giving him a reasonable opportunity of showing cause against the same.

(*3*) A Member nominated under clause (*e*) of sub-section (2) of section 66 may at any time resign his office by writing under his hand addressed to the State Government and the seat of the said Member shall thereupon become vacant.

(*4*) A casual vacancy in the State Advisory Board shall be filled by a fresh nomination and the person nominated to fill the vacancy shall hold office only for the remainder of the term for which the Member in whose place he was so nominated.

(*5*) A Member nominated under sub-clause (*i*) or sub-clause (*iii*) of clause (*e*) of sub-section (2) of section 66 shall be eligible for renomination.

(*6*) the Members nominated under sub-clause (*i*) and sub-clause (*ii*) of clause (*e*) of sub-section (2) of section 66 shall receive such allowances as may be prescribed by the State Government.

Disqualification.

68. (*1*) No person shall be a Member of the State Advisory Board, who—

(*a*) is, or at any time has been, adjudged insolvent or has suspended payment of his debts or has compounded with his creditors, or

(*b*) is of unsound mind and stands so declared by a competent court, or

(*c*) is, or has been, convicted of an offence which, in the opinion of the State Government, involves moral turpitude, or

(*d*) is, or at any time has been, convicted of an offence under this Act, or

(*e*) has so abused in the opinion of the State Government his position as a Member as to render his continuance in the State Advisory Board detrimental to the interests of the general public.

(*2*) No order of removal shall be made by the State Government under this section unless the Member concerned has been given a reasonable opportunity of showing cause against the same.

(*3*) Notwithstanding anything contained in sub-section (*1*) or sub-section (*5*) of section 67, a Member who has been removed under this section shall not be eligible for renomination as a Member.

69. If a Member of the State Advisory Board becomes subject to any of the disqualifications specified in section 68 his seat shall become vacant. Vacation of seats.

70. The State Advisory Board shall meet at least once in every six months and shall observe such rules or procedure in regard to the transaction of business at its meetings as may be prescribed by the State Government. Meetings of State Advisory Board on disability.

71. (*1*) Subject to the provisions of this Act, the State Advisory Board shall be the State-level consultative and advisory body on disability matters, and shall facilitate the continuous evolution of a comprehensive policy for the empowerment of persons with disabilities and the full enjoyment of rights. Functions of State Advisory Board on disability.

(*2*) In particular and without prejudice to the generality of the foregoing provisions, the State Advisory Board on disability shall perform the following functions, namely:—

(*a*) advise the State Government on policies, programmes, legislation and projects with respect to disability;

(*b*) develop a State policy to address issues concerning persons with disabilities;

(*c*) review and coordinate the activities of all Departments of the State Government and other Governmental and non-Governmental Organisations in the State which are dealing with matters relating to persons with disabilities;

(*d*) take up the cause of persons with disabilities with the concerned authorities and the international organisations with a view to provide for schemes and projects for the persons with disabilities in the State plans;

(*e*) recommend steps to ensure accessibility, reasonable accommodation, non-discrimination for persons with disabilities, services and the built environment and their participation in social life on an equal basis with others;

(*f*) monitor and evaluate the impact of laws, policies and programmes designed to achieve full participation of persons with disabilities; and

(*g*) such other functions as may be assigned from time to time by the State Government.

72. The State Government shall constitute District-level Committee on disability to perform such functions as may be prescribed by it. District-level Committee on disability.

73. No act or proceeding of the Central Advisory Board on disability, a State Advisory Board on disability, or a District-level Committee on disability shall be called in question on the ground merely of the existence of any vacancy in or any defect in the constitution of such Board or Committee, as the case may be. Vacancies not to invalidate proceedings.

CHAPTER XII

CHIEF COMMISSIONER AND STATE COMMISSIONER FOR PERSONS WITH DISABILITIES

74. (*1*) The Central Government may, by notification, appoint a Chief Commissioner for Persons with Disabilities (hereinafter referred to as the "Chief Commissioner") for the purposes of this Act. Appointment of Chief Commissioner and Commissioners.

(2) The Central Government may, by notification appoint two Commissioners to assist the Chief Commissioner, of which one Commissioner shall be a persons with disability.

(*3*) A person shall not be qualified for appointment as the Chief Commissioner or Commissioner unless he has special knowledge or practical experience in respect of matters relating to rehabilitation.

(*4*) The salary and allowances payable to and other terms and conditions of service (including pension, gratuity and other retirement benefits) of the Chief Commissioner and Commissioners shall be such as may be prescribed by the Central Government.

(*5*) The Central Government shall determine the nature and categories of officers and other employees required to assist the Chief Commissioner in the discharge of his functions and provide the Chief Commissioner with such officers and other employees as it thinks fit.

(*6*) The officers and employees provided to the Chief Commissioner shall discharge their functions under the general superintendence and control of the Chief Commissioner.

(*7*) The salaries and allowances and other conditions of service of officers and employees shall be such as may be prescribed by the Central Government.

(*8*) The Chief Commissioner shall be assisted by an advisory committee comprising of not more than eleven members drawn from the experts from different disabilities in such manner as may be prescribed by the Central Government.

Functions of Chief Commissioner.

75. (*1*) The Chief Commissioner shall—

(*a*) identify, *suo motu* or otherwise, the provisions of any law or policy, programme and procedures, which are inconsistent with this Act and recommend necessary corrective steps;

(*b*) inquire, *suo motu* or otherwise, deprivation of rights of persons with disabilities and safeguards available to them in respect of matters for which the Central Government is the appropriate Government and take up the matter with appropriate authorities for corrective action;

(*c*) review the safeguards provided by or under this Act or any other law for the time being in force for the protection of rights of persons with disabilities and recommend measures for their effective implementation;

(*d*) review the factors that inhibit the enjoyment of rights of persons with disabilities and recommend appropriate remedial measures;

(*e*) study treaties and other international instruments on the rights of persons with disabilities and make recommendations for their effective implementation;

(*f*) undertake and promote research in the field of the rights of persons with disabilities;

(*g*) promote awareness of the rights of persons with disabilities and the safeguards available for their protection;

(*h*) monitor implementation of the provisions of this Act and schemes, programmes meant for persons with disabilities;

(*i*) monitor utilisation of funds disbursed by the Central Government for the benefit of persons with disabilities; and

(*j*) perform such other functions as the Central Government may assign.

(2) The Chief Commissioner shall consult the Commissioners on any matter while discharging its functions under this Act.

Action of appropriate authorities on recommendation of Chief Commissioner.

76. Whenever the Chief Commissioner makes a recommendation to an authority in pursuance of clause (*b*) of section 75, that authority shall take necessary action on it, and inform the Chief Commissioner of the action taken within three months from the date of receipt of the recommendation:

Provided that where an authority does not accept a recommendation, it shall convey reasons for non-acceptance to the Chief Commissioner within a period of three months, and shall also inform the aggrieved person.

77. *(1)*The Chief Commissioner shall, for the purpose of discharging his functions under this Act, have the same powers of a civil court as are vested in a court under the Code of Civil Procedure, 1908 while trying a suit, in respect of the following matters, namely:— Powers of Chief Commissioner. 5 of 1908.

(*a*) summoning and enforcing the attendance of witnesses;

(*b*) requiring the discovery and production of any documents;

(*c*) requisitioning any public record or copy thereof from any court or office;

(*d*) receiving evidence on affidavits; and

(*e*) issuing commissions for the examination of witnesses or documents.

(*2*) Every proceeding before the Chief Commissioner shall be a judicial proceeding within the meaning of sections 193 and 228 of the Indian Penal Code and the Chief Commissioner shall be deemed to be a civil court for the purposes of section 195 and Chapter XXVI of the Code of Criminal Procedure, 1973. 45 of 1860. 2 of 1974.

78. *(1)* The Chief Commissioner shall submit an annual report to the Central Government and may at any time submit special reports on any matter, which, in his opinion, is of such urgency or importance that it shall not be deferred till submission of the annual report. Annual and special reports by Chief Commissioner.

(*2*) The Central Government shall cause the annual and the special reports of the Chief Commissioner to be laid before each House of Parliament, along with a memorandum of action taken or proposed to be taken on his recommendations and the reasons for non-acceptance the recommendations, if any.

(*3*) The annual and special reports shall be prepared in such form, manner and contain such details as may be prescribed by the Central Government.

79. (*1*) The State Government may, by notification, appoint a State Commissioner for Persons with Disabilities (hereinafter referred to as the "State Commissioner") for the purposes of this Act. Appointment of State Commissioner in States.

(*2*) A person shall not be qualified for appointment as the State Commissioner unless he has special knowledge or practical experience in respect of matters relating to rehabilitation.

(*3*) The salary and allowances payable to and other terms and conditions of service (including pension, gratuity and other retirement benefits) of the State Commissioner shall be such as may be prescribed by the State Government.

(*4*) The State Government shall determine the nature and categories of officers and other employees required to assist the State Commissioner in the discharge of his functions and provide the State Commissioner with such officers and other employees as it thinks fit.

(*5*) The officers and employees provided to the State Commissioner shall discharge his functions under the general superintendence and control of the State Commissioner.

(*6*) The salaries and allowances and other conditions of service of officers and employees shall be such as may be prescribed by the State Government.

(*7*) The State Commissioner shall be assisted by an advisory committee comprising of not more than five members drawn from the experts in the disability sector in such manner as may be prescribed by the State Government.

80. The State Commissioner shall— Functions of State Commissioner.

(*a*) identify, *suo motu* or otherwise, provision of any law or policy, programme and procedures, which are in consistent with this Act, and recommend necessary corrective steps;

(*b*) inquire, *suo motu* or otherwise deprivation of rights of persons with disabilities and safeguards available to them in respect of matters for which the State Government is the appropriate Government and take up the matter with appropriate authorities for corrective action;

(*c*) review the safeguards provided by or under this Act or any other law for the time being in force for the protection of rights of persons with disabilities and recommend measures for their effective implementation;

(*d*) review the factors that inhibit the enjoyment of rights of persons with disabilities and recommend appropriate remedial measures;

(*e*) undertake and promote research in the field of the rights of persons with disabilities;

(*f*) promote awareness of the rights of persons with disabilities and the safeguards available for their protection;

(*g*) monitor implementation of the provisions of this Act and schemes, programmes meant for persons with disabilities;

(*h*) monitor utilisation of funds disbursed by the State Government for the benefits of persons with disabilities; and

(*i*) perform such other functions as the State Government may assign.

Action by appropriate authorities on recommendation of State Commissioner.

81. Whenever the State Commissioner makes a recommendation to an authority in pursuance of clause (*b*) of section 80, that authority shall take necessary action on it, and inform the State Commissioner of the action taken within three months from the date of receipt of the recommendation:

Provided that where an authority does not accept a recommendation, it shall convey reasons for non-acceptance to the State Commissioner for Persons with Disabilities within the period of three months, and shall also inform the aggrieved person.

Powers of State Commissioner.

82. (*1*) The State Commissioner shall, for the purpose of discharging their functions under this Act, have the same powers of a civil court as are vested in a court under the Code of Civil Procedure, 1908 while trying a suit, in respect of the following matters, namely:— 5 of 1908.

(*a*) summoning and enforcing the attendance of witnesses;

(*b*) requiring the discovery and production of any documents;

(*c*) requisitioning any public record or copy thereof from any court or office;

(*d*) receiving evidence on affidavits; and

(*e*) issuing commissions for the examination of witnesses or documents.

(*2*) Every proceeding before the State Commissioner shall be a judicial proceeding within the meaning of sections 193 and 228 of the Indian Penal Code and the State Commissioners shall be deemed to be a civil court for the purposes of section 195 and Chapter XXVI of the Code of Criminal Procedure, 1973. 45 of 1860. 2 of 1974.

Annual and special reports by State Commissioner.

83. (*1*) The State Commissioner shall submit an annual report to the State Government and may at any time submit special reports on any matter, which, in its opinion, is of such urgency or importance that it shall not be deferred till submission of the annual report.

(*2*) The State Government shall cause the annual and the special reports of the State Commissioner for persons with disabilities to be laid before each House of State Legislature where it consists of two Houses or where such Legislature consist of one House, before that House along with a memorandum of action taken or proposed to be taken on the recommendation of the State Commissioner and the reasons for non-acceptance the recommendations, if any.

(*3*) The annual and special reports shall be prepared in such form, manner and contain such details as may be prescribed by the State Government.

CHAPTER XIII

SPECIAL COURT

84. For the purpose of providing speedy trial, the State Government shall, with the concurrence of the Chief Justice of the High Court, by notification, specify for each district, a Court of Session to be a Special Court to try the offences under this Act. Special Court.

85. (*1*) For every Special Court, the State Government may, by notification, specify a Public Prosecutor or appoint an advocate, who has been in practice as an advocate for not less than seven years, as a Special Public Prosecutor for the purpose of conducting cases in that Court. Special Public Prosecutor.

(*2*) The Special Public Prosecutor appointed under sub-section (*1*) shall be entitled to receive such fees or remuneration as may be prescribed by the State Government.

CHAPTER XIV

NATIONAL FUND FOR PERSONS WITH DISABILITIES

86. (*1*) There shall be constituted a Fund to be called the National Fund for persons with disabilities and there shall be credited thereto— National Fund for persons with disabilities.

(*a*) all sums available under the Fund for people with disabilities, constituted *vide* notification No. S.O. 573 (*E*), dated the 11th August, 1983 and the Trust Fund for Empowerment of Persons with Disabilities, constituted *vide* notification No. 30-03/2004-DDII, dated the 21st November, 2006, under the Charitable Endowment

6 of 1890. Act, 1890.

(*b*) all sums payable by banks, corporations, financial institutions in pursuance of judgment dated the 16th April, 2004 of the Hon'ble Supreme Court in Civil Appeal Nos. 4655 and 5218 of 2000;

(*c*) all sums received by way of grant, gifts, donations, benefactions, bequests or transfers;

(*d*) all sums received from the Central Government including grants-in-aid;

(*e*) all sums from such other sources as may be decided by the Central Government.

(*2*) The Fund for persons with disabilities shall be utilised and managed in such manner as may be prescribed.

87. (*1*) The Central Government shall maintain proper accounts and other relevant records and prepare an annual statement of accounts of the Fund including the income and expenditure accounts in such form as may be prescribed in consultation with the Comptroller and Auditor-General of India. Accounts and audit.

(*2*) The accounts of the Fund shall be audited by the Comptroller and Auditor-General of India at such intervals as may be specified by him and any expenditure incurred by him in connection with such audit shall be payable from the Fund to the Comptroller and Auditor-General of India.

(*3*) The Comptroller and Auditor-General of India and any other person appointed by him in connection with the audit of the accounts of the Fund shall have the same rights, privileges and authority in connection with such audit as the Comptroller and Auditor-General of India generally has in connection with the audit of the Government accounts, and in particular, shall have the right to demand production of books of account, connected vouchers and other documents and papers and to inspect any of the offices of the Fund.

(*4*) The accounts of the Fund as certified by the Comptroller and Auditor-General of India or any other person appointed by him in this behalf, together with the audit report thereon, shall be laid before each House of Parliament by the Central Government.

CHAPTER XV

STATE FUND FOR PERSONS WITH DISABILITIES

State Fund for persons with disabilities.

88. (*1*) There shall be constituted a Fund to be called the State Fund for persons with disabilities by a State Government in such manner as may be prescribed by the State Government.

(*2*) The State Fund for persons with disabilities shall be utilised and managed in such manner as may be prescribed by the State Government.

(*3*) Every State Government shall maintain proper accounts and other relevant records of the State Fund for persons with disabilities including the income and expenditure accounts in such form as may be prescribed by the State Government in consultation with the Comptroller and Auditor-General of India.

(*4*) The accounts of the State Fund for persons with disabilities shall be audited by the Comptroller and Auditor-General of India at such intervals as may be specified by him and any expenditure incurred by him in connection with such audit shall be payable from the State Fund to the Comptroller and Auditor-General of India.

(*5*) The Comptroller and Auditor-General of India and any person appointed by him in connection with the audit of the accounts of the State Fund for persons with disabilities shall have the same rights, privileges and authority in connection with such audit as the Comptroller and Auditor-General of India generally has in connection with the audit of the Government accounts, and in particular, shall have right to demand production of books of accounts, connected vouchers and other documents and papers and to inspect any of the offices of the State Fund.

(*6*) The accounts of the State Fund for persons with disabilites as certified by the Comptroller and Auditor-General of India or any other person appointed by him in this behalf together with the audit report thereon shall be laid before each House of the State Legislature where it consists of two Houses or where such Legislature consists of one House before that House.

CHAPTER XVI

OFFENCES AND PENALTIES

Punishment for contravention of provisions of Act or rules or regulations made thereunder.

89. Any person who contravenes any of the provisions of this Act, or of any rule made thereunder shall for first contravention be punishable with fine which may extend to ten thounsand rupees and for any subsequent contravention with fine which shall not be less than fifty thousand rupees but which may extend to five lakh rupees.

Offences by companies.

90. (*1*) Where an offence under this Act has been committed by a company, every person who at the time the offence was committed, was in charge of, and was responsible to, the company for the conduct of the business of the company, as well as the company, shall be deemed to be guilty of the offence and shall be liable to be proceeded against and punished accordingly:

Provided that nothing contained in this sub-section shall render any such person liable to any punishment provided in this Act, if he proves that the offence was committed without his knowledge or that he had exercised all due diligence to prevent the commission of such offence.

(*2*) Notwithstanding anything contained in sub-section (*1*), where an offence under this Act has been committed by a company and it is proved that the offence has been committed with the consent or connivance of, or is attributable to any neglect on the part of any director, manager, secretary or other officer of the company, such director, manager, secretary or other officer shall also be deemed to be guilty of that offence and shall be liable to be proceeded against and punished accordingly.

Explanation.—For the purposes of this section,—

(*a*) "company" means any body corporate and includes a firm or other association of individuals; and

(*b*) "director", in relation to a firm, means a partner in the firm.

Punishment for fraudulently availing any benefit meant for persons with benchmark disabilities.

91. Whoever, fraudulently avails or attempts to avail any benefit meant for persons with benchmark disabilities, shall be punishable with imprisonment for a term which may extend to two years or with fine which may extend to one lakh rupees or with both.

Punishment for offences of atrocities.

92. Whoever,—

(*a*) intentionally insults or intimidates with intent to humiliate a person with disability in any place within public view;

(*b*) assaults or uses force to any person with disability with intent to dishonour him or outrage the modesty of a woman with disability;

(*c*) having the actual charge or control over a person with disability voluntarily or knowingly denies food or fluids to him or her;

(*d*) being in a position to dominate the will of a child or woman with disability and uses that position to exploit her sexually;

(*e*) voluntarily injures, damages or interferes with the use of any limb or sense or any supporting device of a person with disability;

(*f*) performs, conducts or directs any medical procedure to be performed on a woman with disability which leads to or is likely to lead to termination of pregnancy without her express consent except in cases where medical procedure for termination of pregnancy is done in severe cases of disability and with the opinion of a registered medical practitioner and also with the consent of the guardian of the woman with disability,

shall be punishable with imprisonment for a term which shall not be less than six months but which may extend to five years and with fine.

Punishment for failure to furnish information.

93. Whoever, fails to produce any book, account or other documents or to furnish any statement, information or particulars which, under this Act or any order, or direction made or given thereunder, is duty bound to produce or furnish or to answer any question put in pursuance of the provisions of this Act or of any order, or direction made or given thereunder, shall be punishable with fine which may extend to twenty-five thousand rupees in respect of each offence, and in case of continued failure or refusal, with further fine which may extend to one thousand rupees for each day, of continued failure or refusal after the date of original order imposing punishment of fine.

Previous sanction of appropriate Government.

94. No Court shall take cognizance of an offence alleged to have been committed by an employee of the appropriate Government under this Chapter, except with the previous sanction of the appropriate Government or a complaint is filed by an officer authorised by it in this behalf.

Alternative punishments.

95. Where an act or omission constitutes an offence punishable under this Act and also under any other Central or State Act, then, notwithstanding anything contained in any other law for the time being in force, the offender found guilty of such offence shall be liable to punishment only under such Act as provides for punishment which is greater in degree.

CHAPTER XVII

MISCELLANEOUS

Application of other laws not barred.

96. The provisions of this Act shall be in addition to, and not in derogation of, the provisions of any other law for the time being in force.

Protection of action taken in good faith.

97. No suit, prosecution or other legal proceeding shall lie against the appropriate Government or any officer of the appropriate Government or any officer or employee of the Chief Commissioner or the State Commissioner for anything which is in good faith done or intended to be done under this Act or the rules made thereunder.

Power to remove difficulties.

98. *(1)* If any difficulty arises in giving effect to the provisions of this Act, the Central Government may, by order, published in the Official Gazette, make such provisions or give such directions, not inconsistent with the provisions of this Act, as may appear to it to be necessary or expedient for removing the difficulty:

Provided that no such order shall be made under this section after the expiry of the period of two years from the date of commencement of this Act.

(*2*) Every order made under this section shall be laid as soon as may be, after it is made, before each House of Parliament.

Power to amend Schedule.

99. *(1)* On the recommendations made by the appropriate Government or otherwise, if the Central Government is satisfied that it is necessary or expedient so to do, it may, by notification, amend the Schedule and any such notification being issued, the Schedule shall be deemed to have been amended accordingly.

(*2*) Every such notification shall, as soon as possible after it is issued, shall be laid before each House of Parliament.

Power of Central Government to make rules.

100. (*1*) The Central Government may, subject to the condition of previous publication, by notification, make rules for carrying out the provisions of this Act.

(*2*) In particular, and without prejudice to the generality of the foregoing power, such rules may provide for all or any of the following matters, namely:—

(*a*) the manner of constituting the Committee for Research on Disability under sub-section (*2*) of section 6;

(*b*) the manner of notifying the equal opportunity policy under sub-section (*1*) of section 21;

(*c*) the form and manner of maintaining records by every establishment under sub-section (*1*) of section 22;

(*d*) the manner of maintenance of register of complaints by grievance redressal officer under sub-section (*3*) of section 23;

(*e*) the manner of furnishing information and return by establishment to the Special Employment Exchange under section 36;

(*f*) the composition of the Assessment Board under sub-section (*2*) and manner of assessment to be made by the Assessment Board under sub-section (*3*) of section 38;

(*g*) rules for person with disabilites laying down the standards of accessibility under section 40;

(*h*) the manner of application for issuance of certificate of disability under sub-section (*1*) and form of certificate of disability under sub-section (*2*) of section 58;

(*i*) the allowances to be paid to nominated Members of the Central Advisory Board under sub-section (*6*) of section 61;

(*j*) the rules of procedure for transaction of business in the meetings of the Central Advisory Board under section 64;

(*k*) the salaries and allowances and other conditions of services of Chief Commissioner and Commissioners under sub-section (*4*) of section 74;

(*l*) the salaries and allowances and conditions of services of officers and staff of the Chief Commissioner under sub-section (*7*) of section 74;

(*m*) the composition and manner of appointment of experts in the advisory committee under sub-section (*8*) of section 74;

(*n*) the form, manner and content of annual report to be prepared and submitted by the Chief Commissioner under sub-section (*3*) of section 78;

(*o*) the procedure, manner of utilisation and management of the Fund under sub-section (*2*) of section 86; and

(*p*) the form for preparation of accounts of Fund under sub-section (*1*) of section 87.

(*3*) Every rule made under this Act shall be laid, as soon as may be after it is made, before each House of Parliament while it is in session, for a total period of thirty days which may be comprised in one session or in two or more successive sessions, and if, before the expiry of the session immediately following the session or the successive sessions aforesaid, both Houses agree in making any modification in the rule or both Houses agree that the rule should not be made, the rule shall thereafter have effect only in such modified form or be of no effect, as the case may be; so, however, that any such modification or annulment shall be without prejudice to the validity of anything previously done under that rule.

Power of State Government to make rules.

101. (*1*) The State Government may, subject to the condition of previous publication, by notification, make rules for carrying out the provisions of this Act, not later than six months from the date of commencement of this Act.

(*2*) In particular, and without prejudice to the generality of foregoing powers, such rules may provide for all or any of the following matters, namely:—

(*a*) the manner of constituting the Committee for Research on Disablity under sub-section (*2*) of section 5;

(*b*) the manner of providing support of a limited guardian under sub-section (*1*) of section 14;

(*c*) the form and manner of making an application for certificate of registration under sub-section (*1*) of section 51;

(*d*) the facilities to be provided and standards to be met by institutions for grant of certificate of registration under sub-section (*3*) of section 51;

(*e*) the validity of certificate of registration, the form of, and conditions attached to, certificate of registration under sub-section (*4*) of section 51;

(*f*) the period of disposal of application for certificate of registration under sub-section (*7*) of section 51;

(*g*) the period within which an appeal to be made under sub-section (*1*) of section 53;

(*h*) the time and manner of appealing against the order of certifying authority under sub-section (*1*) and manner of disposal of such appeal under sub-section (*2*) of section 59;

(*i*) the allowances to be paid to nominated Members of the State Advisory Board under sub-section (*6*) of section 67;

(*j*) the rules of procedure for transaction of business in the meetings of the State Advisory Board under section 70;

(*k*) the composition and functions of District Level Committee under section 72;

(*l*) salaries, allowances and other conditions of services of the State Commissioner under sub-section (*3*) of section 79;

(*m*) the salaries, allowances and conditions of services of officers and staff of the State Commissioner under sub-section (*3*) of section 79;

(*n*) the composition and manner of appointment of experts in the advisory committee under sub-section (*7*) of section 79;

(*o*) the form, manner and content of annual and special reports to be prepared and submitted by the State Commissioner under sub-section (*3*) of section 83;

(*p*) the fee or remuneration to be paid to the Special Public Prosecutor under sub-section (*2*) of section 85;

(*q*) the manner of constitution of State Fund for persons with disabilities under sub-section (*1*), and the manner of utilisation and management of State Fund under sub-section (*2*) of section 88;

(*r*) the form for preparation of accounts of the State Fund for persons with disabilities under sub-section (*3*) of section 88.

(*3*) Every rule made by the State Government under this Act shall be laid, as soon as may be after it is made, before each House of the State Legislature where it consists of two Houses, or where such State Legislature consists of one House, before that House.

Repeal and savings.

102. (*1*) The Persons with Disabilities (Equal Opportunity Protection of Rights and Full Participation) Act, 1995 is hereby repealed. 1 of 1996.

(*2*) Notwithstanding the repeal of the said Act, anything done or any action taken under the said Act, shall be deemed to have been done or taken under the corresponding provisions of this Act.

THE SCHEDULE

[*See* clause (*zc*) of section 2]

SPECIFIED DISABILITY

1. Physical disability.—

A. Locomotor disability (a person's inability to execute distinctive activities associated with movement of self and objects resulting from affliction of musculoskeletal or nervous system or both), including—

(*a*) "leprosy cured person" means a person who has been cured of leprosy but is suffering from—

(*i*) loss of sensation in hands or feet as well as loss of sensation and paresis in the eye and eye-lid but with no manifest deformity;

(*ii*) manifest deformity and paresis but having sufficient mobility in their hands and feet to enable them to engage in normal economic activity;

(*iii*) extreme physical deformity as well as advanced age which prevents him/her from undertaking any gainful occupation, and the expression "leprosy cured" shall construed accordingly;

(*b*) "cerebral palsy" means a Group of non-progressive neurological condition affecting body movements and muscle coordination, caused by damage to one or more specific areas of the brain, usually occurring before, during or shortly after birth;

(*c*) "dwarfism" means a medical or genetic condition resulting in an adult height of 4 feet 10 inches (147 centimeters) or less;

(*d*) "muscular dystrophy" means a group of hereditary genetic muscle disease that weakens the muscles that move the human body and persons with multiple dystrophy have incorrect and missing information in their genes, which prevents them from making the proteins they need for healthy muscles. It is characterised by progressive skeletal muscle weakness, defects in muscle proteins, and the death of muscle cells and tissue;

(*e*) "acid attack victims" means a person disfigured due to violent assaults by throwing of acid or similar corrosive substance.

B. Visual impairment—

(*a*) "blindness" means a condition where a person has any of the following conditions, after best correction—

(*i*) total absence of sight; or

(*ii*) visual acuity less than 3/60 or less than 10/200 (Snellen) in the better eye with best possible correction; or

(*iii*) limitation of the field of vision subtending an angle of less than 10 degree.

(*b*) "low-vision" means a condition where a person has any of the following conditons, namely:—

(*i*) visual acuity not exceeding 6/18 or less than 20/60 upto 3/60 or upto 10/200 (Snellen) in the better eye with best possible corrections; or

34THE GAZETTE OF INDIA EXTRAORDINARY[PART II—

(*ii*) limitation of the field of vision subtending an angle of less than 40 degree up to 10 degree.

C. Hearing impairment—

(*a*) "deaf" means persons having 70 DB hearing loss in speech frequencies in both ears;

(*b*) "hard of hearing" means person having 60 DB to 70 DB hearing loss in speech frequencies in both ears;

D. "speech and language disability" means a permanent disability arising out of conditions such as laryngectomy or aphasia affecting one or more components of speech and language due to organic or neurological causes.

2. Intellectual disability, a condition characterised by significant limitation both in intellectual functioning (rasoning, learning, problem solving) and in adaptive behaviour which covers a range of every day, social and practical skills, including—

(*a*) "specific learning disabilities" means a heterogeneous group of conditions wherein there is a deficit in processing language, spoken or written, that may manifest itself as a difficulty to comprehend, speak, read, write, spell, or to do mathematical calculations and includes such conditions as perceptual disabilities, dyslexia, dysgraphia, dyscalculia, dyspraxia and developmental aphasia;

(*b*) "autism spectrum disorder" means a neuro-developmental condition typically appearing in the first three years of life that significantly affects a person's ability to communicate, understand relationships and relate to others, and is frequently associated with unusal or stereotypical rituals or behaviours.

3. Mental behaviour,—

"mental illness" means a substantial disorder of thinking, mood, perception, orientation or memory that grossly impairs judgment, behaviour, capacity to recognise reality or ability to meet the ordinary demands of life, but does not include retardation which is a conditon of arrested or incomplete development of mind of a person, specially characterised by subnormality of intelligence.

4. Disability caused due to—

(*a*) chronic neurological conditions, such as—

(*i*) "multiple sclerosis" means an inflammatory, nervous system disease in which the myelin sheaths around the axons of nerve cells of the brain and spinal cord are damaged, leading to demyelination and affecting the ability of nerve cells in the brain and spinal cord to communicate with each other;

(*ii*) "parkinson's disease" means a progressive disease of the nervous system marked by tremor, muscular rigidity, and slow, imprecise movement, chiefly affecting middle-aged and elderly people associated with degeneration of the basal ganglia of the brain and a deficiency of the neurotransmitter dopamine.

(*b*) Blood disorder—

(*i*) "haemophilia" means an inheritable disease, usually affecting only male but transmitted by women to their male children, characterised by loss or impairment of the normal clotting ability of blood so that a minor would may result in fatal bleeding;

(*ii*) "thalassemia" means a group of inherited disorders characterised by reduced or absent amounts of haemoglobin.

(*iii*) "sickle cell disease" means a hemolytic disorder characterised by chronic anemia, painful events, and various complications due to associated tissue and organ damage; "hemolytic" refers to the destruction of the cell membrane of red blood cells resulting in the release of hemoglobin.

5. Multiple Disabilities (more than one of the above specified disabilities) including deaf blindness which means a condition in which a person may have combination of hearing and visual impairments causing severe communication, developmental, and educational problems.

6. Any other category as may be notified by the Central Government.

DR. G. NARAYANA RAJU,
Secretary to the Govt. of India.

UPLOADED BY THE GENERAL MANAGER, GOVERNMENT OF INDIA PRESS, MINTO ROAD, NEW DELHI-110002 AND PUBLISHED BY THE CONTROLLER OF PUBLICATIONS, DELHI-110054.

GMGIPMRND—4011GI(S3)—28-12-2016.

RPWD Rules 2017 and Amendment Rules 2019, 2020 & 2023

The Rights of Persons with Disabilities Rules, 2017 (as updated)

Published vide Notification No. G.S.R. 591(E), dated 15th June, 2017

Inludes the following:

1. Insertion of Chapter V A vide the Rights of Persons with Disabilities (Amendment) Rules, 2019 published vide notification No. G.S.R. 209(E), dated 08th March2019;

2. Insertion vide G.S.R. 181(E)Rights of Persons with Disabilities (Amendment) Rules, 2020:

3. Insertion of ICT Standards in Section 15 videRPWD (Amendment) Rules 2023 issued vide G.S.R. 359(E) dated 10 May 2023

4. Insertion of Hamonised Guidelines on Universal Accessibility 2021 replacing the HG 2016 in15(1)(a) vide RPWD (Amendment) Rules 2023 issued vide G.S.R. 413(E) dated 05 June 2023}

[Department of Empowerment of Persons with Disabilities (Divyangjan)]

Ministry of Social Justice and Empowerment

G.S.R. 591(E). - Whereas a draft of the Rights of Persons with Disabilities Rules, 2017 was published as required by sub-sections (1) and (2) of section 100 of the Rights of

Persons with Disabilities Act, 2016 (49 of 2016) in the Gazette of India, Extraordinary, Part-II, Section 3, Sub-section (i) *vide* number G.S.R. 398 (E), dated the 21st April, 2017, inviting objections and suggestions from all persons likely to be affected thereby, before the expiry of thirty days from the date on which the copies of the Official Gazette containing the said notification were made available to the public;

And whereas the copies of the *Official Gazette* in which the said notification was published were made available to the public on the 22nd April, 2017;

And whereas objections and suggestions received from the public on the said draft rules were considered by the Central Government;

Now, therefore, in exercise of powers conferred by sub-sections (1) and (2) of section 100 of the Rights of Persons with Disabilities Act, 2016 (49 of 2016), the Central Government hereby makes the following rules, namely:-

CHAPTER I
Preliminary

1. Short title, extent and commencement. - (1) These rules may be called the Rights of Persons with Disabilities Rules, 2017.

(2) They extend to the whole of India.

(3) They shall come into force from the date of their publication in the Official Gazette.

2. Definitions. - (1) In these rules, unless the context otherwise requires,-

(a) *"Act"* means the Rights of Persons with Disabilities Act, 2016 (49 of 2016);

(b) *"certificate"* means a certificate of disability issued under section 57 of the Act;

(c) *"Form"* means a form appended to these rules.

(2) Words and expressions used herein and not defined but defined in the Act shall have the meanings respectively assigned to them in the Act.

CHAPTER II
Rights and Entitlements

3. Establishment not to discriminate on the ground of disability. - (1) The head of the establishment shall ensure that the provision of sub-section (3) of section 3 of the Act are not misused to deny any right or benefit to persons with disabilities covered under the Act.

(2) If the head of the Government establishment or a private establishment employing twenty or more persons receives a complaint from an aggrieved persons regarding discrimination on the ground of disability, he shall -

(a) initiate action in accordance with the provisions of the Act; or

(b) inform the aggrieved person in writing as to how the impugned act or omission is a proportionate means of achieving a legitimate aim.

(3) If the aggrieved person submits a complaint to the Chief Commissioner or State Commissioner for Persons with Disabilities, as the case may be, the complaint shall be disposed of within a period of sixty days:

Provided that in exceptional cases, the Chief Commissioner or State Commissioner may dispose of such complaint within thirty days.

(4) No establishment shall compel a person with disability to partly or fully pay the costs incurred for reasonable accommodation.

4. Central Committee for Research on Disability. - (1) The Central Committee for Research on Disability shall consist of the following persons, namely:-

(i) an eminent person having vast experience in the field of science or medicine, to be nominated by the Central Government, *ex officio* - Chairperson;

(ii) nominee of the Director General of Health Services not below the rank of Deputy Director General - Member;

(iii) four persons drawn from National Institutes representing physical, visual, hearing and intellectual disabilities, to be nominated by the Central Government - Members;

(iv) five persons as representatives of the registered organisations, from each of the five groups of specified disabilities in the Schedule to the Act, to be nominated by the Central Government - Members:

Provided that at least one representative of the registered organizations is a woman;

(v) the Director, Department of Empowerment of Persons with Disabilities, New Delhi shall be the Member Secretary.

(2) The Chairperson may invite any expert as a special invitee.

(3) The term of office of the nominated members shall be for a period of three years from the date on which they enter upon office, and the nominated member shall be eligible for re-nomination for one more term.

(4) One half of the members shall constitute the quorum for the meeting.

(5) The non-official members and special invitees shall be entitled for travelling allowance and daily allowance as admissible to a Group "A" officer of the Central Government.

(6) The Central Government may provide the Committee with such clerical and other staff as it deems necessary.

5. Person with disability not to be a subject of research. - No person with disability shall be a subject of research except when the research involves physical impact on his body.

6. Procedure to be followed by Executive Magistrate. - For the purposes of dealing with the complaints under section 7 of the Act, the Executive Magistrate shall follow the procedure provided in sections 133 to 143 of the Code of Criminal Procedure, 1973 (2 of 1974).

CHAPTER III

Nodal Officer in the District Education Office

7. There shall be a nodal officer in the District Education Office to deal with all matters relating to admission of children with disabilities and the facilities to be provided to them in schools in accordance with the provisions of sections 16 and 31 of the Act.

CHAPTER IV

Employment

8. Manner of publication of equal opportunity policy. - (1) Every establishment shall publish equal opportunity policy for persons with disabilities.

(2) The establishment shall display the equal opportunity policy preferably on their website, failing which, at conspicuous places in their premises.

(3) The equal opportunity policy of a private establishment having twenty or more employees and the Government establishments shall *inter alia*, contain the following, namely:-

---

(a) facility and amenity to be provided to the persons with disabilities to enable them to effectively discharge their duties in the establishment;

(b) list of posts identified suitable for persons with disabilities in the establishment;

(c) the manner of selection of persons with disabilities for various posts, post-recruitment and pre-promotion training, preference in transfer and posting, special leave, preference in allotment of residential accommodation if any, and other facilities;

(d) provisions for assistive devices, barrier-free accessibility and other provisions for persons with disabilities;

(e) appointment of liaison officer by the establishment to look after the recruitment of persons with disabilities and provisions of facilities and amenities for such employees.

(4) The equal opportunity policy of the private establishment having less than twenty employees shall contain facilities and amenities to be provided to the persons with disabilities to enable them to effectively discharge their duties in the establishment.

9. Form and manner of maintaining records by the establishments. - (1) Every establishment covered under sub-rule (3) of rule 8 shall maintain records containing the following particulars, namely:-

(a) the number of persons with disabilities who are employed and the date from when they are employed;

(b) the name, gender and address of persons with disabilities;

(c) the nature of disability of such persons;

(d) the nature of work being rendered by such employed person with disability; and

(e) the kind of facilities being provided to such persons with disabilities.

(2) Every establishment shall produce for inspection on demand, records maintained under these rules, to the

authorities under this Act and shall supply such information which may be required for the purpose of ascertaining whether the provisions have been complied with.

10. Manner of maintenance of register of complaints by the Government establishments. - (1) Every Government establishment shall appoint an officer not below the rank of a Gazetted Officer as Grievance Redressal Officer:

Provided that where it is not possible to appoint any Gazetted Officer, the Government establishment may appoint the senior most Officer as a Grievance Redressal Officer.

(2) The Grievance Redressal Officer shall maintain a register of complaints of persons with disabilities with the following particulars, namely:-

(a) date of complaint;
(b) name of complainant;
(c) name of the person who is enquiring the complaint;
(d) place of incident;
(e) the name of establishment or person against whom the complaint is made;
(f) gist of the complaint;
(g) documentary evidence, if any;
(h) date of disposal by the Grievance Redressal Officer;
(i) details of disposal of the appeal by the district level committee; and
(j) any other information.

CHAPTER V

Vacancies for Persons with Benchmark Disabilities

11. Computation of vacancies. - (1) For the purposes of computation of vacancies, four percent of the total number of vacancies including vacancies arising in the identified and non-identified posts in the cadre strength in each group of posts shall be taken into account by the appropriate Government for the persons with benchmark disabilities:

Provided that the reservation in promotion shall be in accordance with the instructions issued by the appropriate Government from time to time.

(2) Every Government establishment shall maintain a vacancy based roster for the purpose of calculation of vacancies for persons with benchmark disabilities in the cadre strength as per the instructions issued by the appropriate Government from time to time.

(3) While making advertisement to fill up vacancies, every Government establishment shall indicate the number of vacancies reserved for each class of persons with benchmark disabilities in accordance with the provisions of section 34 of the Act.

(4) The reservation for persons with disabilities in accordance with the provisions of section 34 of the Act shall be horizontal and the vacancies for persons with benchmark disabilities shall be maintained as a separate class.

12. Interchange of vacancies. - The Government establishment shall interchange vacancies in accordance with the provisions of section 34 of the Act, only if due process of recruitment to fill up the vacancies reserved for persons with benchmark disabilities has been complied with.

13. Submission of Returns on Vacancies. - (1) Every Government establishment shall furnish to the local special employment exchange returns in Form - I once in every six months for the period from 1st April to 30th September and from 1st October to 31st March, and in Form -II once in every two years.

(2) The six monthlyreturn shall be furnished within thirty days of the respective dates which is, 31st March and, 30th September of every financial year.

(3) The two yearly return shall be furnished within thirty days of the closing of every alternate financial year:

Provided that the first two yearly returns shall be furnished for the financial year closing on 31st March, 2019.

14. Form in which record to be kept by an employer. - Every Government establishment shall maintain the record of employees with disabilities in Form - III.

CHAPTER V A

(Inserted vide Rights of Persons with Disabilities (Amendment) Rules, 2019)

14A. (1) The State Governments or Union Territory Administrations shall notify the authority to whom a person with benchmark disability can apply for the high support requirement as per sub-section (1) of Section 38 of the Act.

(2) Only the persons with benchmark disabilities having permanent certificate of disability shall be eligible for applying for high support requirement.

(3) The State Governments shall constitute Assessment Board at the District level or Division level based on the number of persons with benchmark disabilities comprising the following:-

(a) District Chief Medical Officer or Civil Surgeon or Medical Superintendent....Chairperson;

(b) District Social Welfare Officer.........Member;

(c) Five rehabilitation specialists [Physical Medicine and Rehabilitation or Orthopaedic specialist, ENT specialist, Ophthalmologist, General Physician (if the applicant is 18 years or above) or Pediatrician (if the applicant is less than 18 years), Psychiatrist]...........Members;

(d) Occupational therapist or speech therapist or Clinical Psychologist or Physiotherapist (as per requirement)........... Member;

(e) Any other expert as the Chairperson deems appropriate.........Member.

(4) The authority notified under sub-rule (1) shall refer every case to the Assessment Board for assessment of applicant's high support requirement.

(5) The Assessment Board shall invite the applicant of high support requirements for assessment and may, if necessary, seek clinical assessment.

(6) The Assessment Board shall assess the applicant on the basis of the six parameters (a) to (f) and assign scores on the basis of the 100 point graded weightage indicated below:-

Parameters		Weightage
(a) Severity of physical disability (Max. weightage – 25)	(a) 40% - 59% (b) 60% - 79% (c) 80% - 100%	15 20 25
(b) Severity of mental/ developmental disability (which restricts the person to take any informed decision) (Max. weightage – 25)	(a) 40% - 59% (b) 60% - 79% (c) 80% - 100%	15 20 25
(c) The extent to which daily activities in a person is hampered (Max. weightage – 35)	(i)Bathing, Brushing, combing, Dressing (ii) Toilet hygiene (getting to the toilet, cleaning oneself, getting backup etc) (iii) Functional mobility (ability to work, get in and out of bed, get in and out of a chair, moving from one place to other while performing activities) (iv) Self-feeding (not including cooking)	10 10 10 5
(d) Cognitive Abilities like ability to take safety measures to use transport, logistics, gadgets, not to get lost (Max. weightage – 5)	-	5
(e) Environmental Barriers like access to health care or support systems for	-	5

rehabilitation or health needs (Max. weightage – 5)		
(f) Socio-economic status (Max. weightage – 5)	APL BPL	0 5
Total		100

(7) Any person with benchmark disability with a score 60 out of 100 point mentioned in sub-rule (6) may be recommended by the Assessment Board for high support needs.

(8) The Assessment Board shall submit its recommendations to the authority notified under sub-rule (1) within a period of 90 days from the date of receiving request for assessment from the said authority.

(9) The State Government or Union Territory Administrations may develop dedicated schemes to provide high support to such persons with benchmark disabilities.

(10) The authority notified under sub-rule (1) shall consider the application for high support requirement on the basis of the recommendations of the Assessment Board keeping in view the schemes or programmes of the respective State Governments or Union Territory Administrations, as the case may be.

CHAPTER VI
Accessibility

15. Rules for Accessibility. - (1) Every establishment shall comply with the following standards relating to physical environment, transport and information and communication technology, namely :-(a) ~~standard for public buildings as specified in the Harmonised Guidelines and Space Standards for Barrier Free Built Environment for Persons With Disabilities and Elderly Persons as issued by the Government of India, Ministry of Urban Development in March, 2016;~~standard for public buildings as specified in the Harmonised Guidelines and Standards for Universal Accessibility in India – 2021, notified by the Government of India in the Ministry of Housing and Urban Affairs, vide notification number O-17/4/2022-works-3-UD dated the 18th October, 2022, as amended from time to time. **(sub para 15(1)(a) replaced by Rights of Persons with Disabilities (Amendment) Rules 2023 issued vide G.S.R. 413(E) dated 05 June 2023)**

(b) standard for Bus Body Code for transportation system as specified in the notification of the Government of India in the Ministry of Road Transport and Highways, *vide* number G.S.R. 895(E), dated the 20th September, 2016;

(c) Information and Communication Technology -

(i) website standard as specified in the guidelines for Indian Government websites, as adopted by Department of Administrative Reforms and Public Grievances, Government of India;

(ii) documents to be placed on websites shall be in Electronic Publication (ePUB) or Optical Character Reader (OCR) based Pdf format:

(iii Websites, apps, information and communication technology based public facilities and services, electronic goods and equipment which are meant for everyday use, information and communication technology based consumer products and accessories for general use with persons with disabilities, and other products and services which are based on information and communication technology, shall comply with the Indian standards IS 17802 (Part 1), 2021 and IS 17802 (Part 2), 2022, published by the Bureau of Indian Standards vide notification numbers HQ-PUB013/1/2020-PUB-BIS(278), dated the 24th December, 2021 and HQ-PUB013/1/2020-PUB-BIS(358), dated the 4th May, 2022, respectively as amended from time to time ***[sub para (iii) inserted vide RPWD Amenment rules 2023 issued vide G.S.R. 359(E) dated 10 May 2023]***

Provided that the standard of accessibility in respect of other services and facilities shall be specified by the Central Government within a period of six months from the date of notification of these rules.

(2) The respective Ministries and Departments shall ensure compliance of the standards of accessibility specified under this rule through the concerned domain regulators or otherwise.

16. Review of Accessibility Standards. - The Central Government shall review from time to time the accessibility standards notified based on the latest scientific knowledge and technology.

CHAPTER VII

Certificate of Disability

17. Application for certificate of disability. - (1) Any person with specified disability may apply in Form -IV for a certificate of disability and submit the application to -

(a) a medical authority or any other notified competent authority to issue such a certificate in the district of residence of the applicant as mentioned in the proof of residence in the application; or

(b) the concerned medical authority in a government hospital where he may be undergoing or may have undergone treatment in connection with his disability:

Provided that where a person with disability is a minor or suffering from intellectual disability or any other disability which renders him unfit or unable to make such an application himself, the application on his behalf may be made by his legal guardian or by any organisation registered under the Act having the minor under its care.

(2) The application shall be accompanied by -

a) proof of residence;
b) two recent passport size photographs; and
c) aadhaar number or aadhaar enrollment number, if any.

Note. - No other proof of residence shall be demanded from the applicant who has aadhaar or aadhaar enrollment number.

18. Issue of certificate of disability. - (1) On receipt of an application under rule 17, the medical authority or any other notified competent authority shall, verify the information as provided by the applicant and shall assess the disability in terms of the relevant guidelines issued by the Central Government and after satisfying himself that the applicant is a person with disability, issue a certificate of disability in his favour in Form V, VI and VII, as the case may be.

(2) The medical authority shall issue the certificate of disability within a month from the date of receipt of the application.

(3) The medical authority shall, after due examination -

- (i) issue a permanent certificate of disability in cases where there are no chances of variation of disability over time in the degree of disability; or
- (ii) issue a certificate of disability indicating the period of validity, in cases where there is any chance of variation over time in the degree of disability.

(4) If an applicant is found ineligible for issue of certificate of disability, the medical authority shall convey the reasons to him in writing under Form VIII within a period of one month from the date of receipt of the application.

(5) The State Government and Union territory Administration shall ensure that the certificate of disability is granted on online platform from such date as may be notified by the Central Government.

19. Certificate issued under rule 18 to be generally valid for all purposes. - A person to whom the certificate issued under rule 18 shall be entitled to apply for facilities, concessions and benefits admissible for persons with disabilities under schemes of the Government and of non-Governmental organizations funded by the Government.

20. Validity of certificate of disability issued under the repealed Act. -

The certificate of disability issued under the Persons with Disabilities (Equal Opportunities, Protection of Rights and Full Participation) Act, 1995 (1 of 1996) shall continue to be valid after commencement of the Act for the period specified therein.

CHAPTER VIII

Central Advisory Board on Disability

21. Allowances for the members of the Central Advisory Board. - (1) The non-official members of the Central Advisory Board, in Delhi, shall be paid an allowance of rupees two thousand per day for each day of the actual meeting.

(2) The non-official members of the Central Advisory Board, not residing in Delhi shall be paid daily allowance and travelling allowance for each day of the actual meeting at the rate admissible to a Group "A" officer of the Central Government:

Provided that in case a Member of Parliament who is a Member of the Central Advisory Board, the daily allowance and travelling allowance shall be paid at the rate admissible to him as Member of Parliament when the Parliament is not in session and on production of a certificate by the Member that he has not drawn any such allowance for the same journey and halts from any other Government source.

(3) The official member of the Central Advisory Board shall be paid daily allowance and travelling allowance, at the rate admissible under the relevant rules of the respective Government under whom he is serving on production of a certificate by him that he has not drawn any such allowance for the same journey and halts from any other Government source.

22. Notice of meeting. - (1) The meeting of the Central Advisory Board on disability shall ordinarily be held in New Delhi on such dates as may be fixed by the Chairperson:

Provided that it shall meet at least once in every six months.

(2) The Chairperson shall, on the written request of not less than ten members of the Central Advisory Board, call a special meeting of the Board.

(3) The Member -Secretary shall give fifteen clear days' notice of an ordinary meeting and five clear days' notice of a special meeting specifying the time and the place at which such meeting is to be held and the business to be transacted thereat.

(4) The Member-Secretary may give notice to the members by delivering the same by messenger or sending it by registered post to his last known place of residence or business or by email or in such other manner as the Chairperson may, in the circumstances of the case, think fit.

(5) No member shall be entitled to bring forward for the consideration of the meeting, any matter of which he has not given ten clear days' notice to the Member- Secretary, unless the Chairperson may permit him to do so.

(6) The Central Advisory Board may adjourn its meeting from day to day or to any particular day.

(7) Where a meeting of the Central Advisory Board is adjourned from day to day, the Member-Secretary shall give notice of such adjourned meeting at the place where the meeting is adjourned, if held, by messenger and it shall not be necessary to give notice of the adjourned meeting to other members.

(8) Where a meeting of the Central Advisory Board is adjourned not from day to day but from the day on which the meeting is to be held to another day, notice of such meeting shall be given to all the members as provided in sub-rule (4).

23. Presiding officer. - The Chairperson shall preside over every meeting of the Central Advisory Board and in his absence, the Vice-Chairperson shall preside, but when both the Chairperson and the Vice-Chairperson are absent from any meeting, the members present shall elect one of the members to preside over that meeting.

24. Quorum. - (1) One-third of the total members of the Central Advisory Board shall form the quorum for any meeting.

(2) If time fixed for any meeting or during the course of any meeting, less than one-third of the total members are present, the Chairperson may adjourn the meeting to such hours on the following or on some other future date as he may fix.

(3) No quorum shall be necessary for the adjourned meeting.

(4) No matter, which had not been on the agenda of the ordinary or the special meeting, as the case may be, shall be discussed at adjourned meeting.

25. Minutes. - (1) The Member-Secretary shall maintain the record containing the names of members who attended the meeting and of the proceedings at the meetings in a book to be kept for that purpose.

(2) The minutes of the previous meeting shall be read at the beginning of the every succeeding meeting, and shall be confirmed and signed by the presiding officer at such meeting.

(3) The proceedings shall be open to inspection by any member at the office of the Member-Secretary during office hours.

26. Business to be transacted at meeting. - Except with the permission of the presiding officer, no business which is not entered in the agenda or of which notice has not been given by a member under sub-rule (5) of rule 22 shall be transacted at any meeting.

27. Agenda for the meeting of the Central Advisory Board. - (1) The business of the meeting shall be transacted in the order in which it is entered in the agenda, unless otherwise resolved in the meeting with the permission of the presiding officer.

(2) At the beginning of the meeting or after the conclusion of the debate on a motion during the meeting, the presiding officer or a member may suggest a change in the order of

business as entered in the agenda and if the Chairperson agrees, such a change shall take place.

28. Decision by majority. - All questions considered at a meeting of the Committee shall be decided by a majority of votes of the members present and voting and in the event of equality of votes, the Chairperson, or in the absence of the Chairperson, the Vice-Chairperson or in the absence of both the member presiding at the meeting, as the case may be, shall have a second or casting vote.

29. No proceeding to be invalid due to vacancy or any defect. - No proceeding of the Central Advisory Board shall be invalid by reason of existence of any vacancy in or any defect in the constitution of the Board.

CHAPTER IX

Chief Commissioner and Commissioner for Persons with Disabilities

30. Qualification for appointment of Chief Commissioner. - No person shall be eligible for appointment as Chief Commissioner, unless -

(a) he is a Graduate from a recognized University:

Provided that preference shall be given to persons having recognised degree or diploma in social work or law or management or human rights or rehabilitation or education of persons with disabilities;

(b) he is having experience of at least twenty-five years in a Group "A" level post in the Central Government or a State Government or a public sector undertaking or a semi Government or an autonomous body dealing with disability related matters or social sector or as a senior level functionary in registered national and international voluntary organizations in the field of disability or social development:

Provided that out of the total of twenty-five years of experience, he should have at least three years of experience in the field of rehabilitation or empowerment of persons with disabilities; and

(c) he has not attained the age of sixty years as on 1st January of the year of recruitment.

Note. - If he is in the service under the Central Government or a State Government, he shall seek retirement from such service before his appointment to the post.

31. Qualification for appointment of Commissioner. - No person shall be eligible for appointment as Commissioner, unless-

(a) he is a Graduate from a recognized University:

Provided that preference shall be given to persons having recognised degree or diploma in social work or law or management or human rights or rehabilitation or education of persons with disabilities.

(b) he is having at least twenty years experience in a Group "A" level post in the Central Government or a State Government or a public sector undertaking or a semi Government or an autonomous body dealing with disability related matters or social sector or as senior level functionary in registered national and international voluntary organizations in the field of disability or social development; and

(c) he has not attained the age of fifty-six years as on 1st January of the year of recruitment.

"(b) he is having at least twenty years experience in a Group "A" level post in the Central Government or a State Government or a public sector undertaking or a semi Government or an autonomous body dealing with disability related matters or social sector or as senior level functionary in registered national and international voluntary organisations in the field of disability or social development:

Provided that out of the total of twenty years of experience, he should have at least three years of experience in the field of rehabilitation or empowerment of persons with disabilities; and

(c) he is less than fifty-six years of age as on the 1st January of the year of recruitment." (*substituted by Rights of Persons with Disabilities (Amendment) Rules, 2020.*)

32. Method of appointment of the Chief Commissioner and Commissioner. - (1) The Central Government shall, six months before the post of Chief Commissioner is due to fall vacant, advertise in at least two national level dailies each in English and Hindi inviting applications for the post from eligible candidates fulfilling the qualifications specified in rules 30 and 31.

(2) A search-cum-selection committee shall be constituted to recommend a panel of three suitable candidates for the post of the Chief Commissioner or the Commissioner.

(3) The search-cum-selection committee shall be constituted in accordance with the instructions issued by the Government from time to time.

(4) The panel recommended by the committee may consist of persons from amongst those who have applied in response to the advertisement mentioned in sub-rule (1) and other eligible persons whom the Committee may consider suitable.

(5) The Central Government shall appoint one of the candidates recommended by the search-cum-selection committee as the Chief Commissioner or the Commissioner.

33. Term of the Chief Commissioner and Commissioner. - (1) The term of office of Chief Commissioner shall be for a period of three years from the date on which he assumes office, or till he attains the age of sixty-five years, whichever is earlier.

(2) The term of office of the Commissioner shall be for a period of three years and may be extended for a period of another two years or till he attains the age of sixty years, whichever is earlier.

(3) A person may serve as Chief Commissioner or Commissioner for a maximum period of two terms subject to the condition that he has not attained the age of sixty-five years, or sixty years, respectively.

34. Salary and allowances of the Chief Commissioner and Commissioner. - (1) The Chief Commissioner shall be entitled for the salary and allowances as admissible to a Secretary to the Government of India.

(2) The Commissioner shall be entitled for the salary and allowances as admissible to a Additional Secretary to the Government of India.

(3) Where a Chief Commissioner or the Commissioner being a retired Government servant or a retired employee of any institution or autonomous body funded by the Government, is in receipt of pension in respect of such previous service, the salary admissible to him under these rules shall be reduced by the amount of the pension, and if he had received in lieu of a portion of the pension, the commuted value thereof, by the amount of such commuted portion of the pension.

35. Other terms and conditions of service of the Chief Commissioner and Commissioner. - (1) The Chief Commissioner and the Commissioner shall be entitled to such leave as is admissible to a Government servant under the Central Civil Service (Leave) Rules, 1972.

(2) The Chief Commissioner and the Commissioner shall be entitled to such leave travel concession as is admissible to a Group "A" officer under the Central Civil Services (Leave Travel Concession) Rules, 1988.

(3) The Chief Commissioner and the Commissioner shall be entitled to such medical benefits as is admissible to a Group "A" officer under the Central Government Health Scheme.

36. Resignation and removal. - (1) The Chief Commissioner and the Commissioner may, by notice in writing, under his hand, addressed to the Central Government, resign from the office:

Provided that he shall continue in the office till his resignation is accepted.

(2) The Central Government may remove a person from the office of the Chief Commissioner and the Commissioner, if he -

(a) becomes an undischarged insolvent;

(b) engages during his term of office in any paid employment or activity outside the duties of his office;

(c) is convicted or sentenced to imprisonment for an offence which in the opinion of the Central Government involves moral turpitude;

(d) is in the opinion of the Central Government, unfit to continue in office by reason of infirmity of mind or body or serious default in the performance of his functions as laid down in the Act;

(e) without obtaining leave of absence from the Central Government, remains absent from duty for a consecutive period of fifteen days or more; or

(f) has, in the opinion of the Central Government, so abused the position of the Chief Commissioner and Commissioner as to render his continuance in office detrimental to the interest of persons with disability:

Provided that no person shall be removed under this rule except after following the procedure, *mutatis mutandis*, applicable for removal of a Group "A" employee of the Central Government.

(3) The Central Government may suspend the Chief Commissioner and the Commissioner, in respect of whom proceedings for removal have been commenced in accordance with sub-rule (2), pending conclusion of such proceedings.

37. Residuary provision. - The conditions of service of the Chief Commissioner and the Commissioner in respect of which no express provision has been made in these rules shall be determined by the rules and orders for the time being applicable to the Secretary and Additional Secretary to the Government of India, as the case may be.

38. Procedure to be followed by Chief Commissioner and Commissioner. - (1) An aggrieved person may present a complaint containing the following particulars in person or by his agent to the Chief Commissioner or the Commissioner or send it by registered post or by email addressed to the Chief Commissioner or the Commissioner, namely:-

(a) the name, description and the address of the aggrieved person;

(b) the name, description and the address of the opposite party or parties, as the case may be, so far as they may be ascertained;

(c) the facts relating to complaint and when and where it arose;

(d) documents in support of the allegations contained in the complaint; and

(e) the relief which the aggrieved person claims.

(2) The Chief Commissioner or the Commissioner on receipt of a complaint shall refer a copy of the complaint to the opposite party or parties mentioned in the complaint, directing him to give his version of the case within a period of thirty days or such extended period not exceeding fifteen

days as may be granted by the Chief Commissioner or the Commissioner.

(3) On the date of hearing or any other date to which hearing could be adjourned, the parties or their agents shall appear before the Chief Commissioner or the Commissioner.

(4) Where the aggrieved person or his agent fails to appear before the Chief Commissioner or the Commissioner on such days, the Chief Commissioner or the Commissioner may either dismiss the complaint on default or decide on merits.

(5) Where the opposite party or his agent fails to appear on the date of hearing, the Chief Commissioner or the Commissioner may take such necessary action under section 77 of the Act as he deems fit for summoning and enforcing the attendance of the opposite party.

(6) The Chief Commissioner or the Commissioner may dispose of the complaint *ex-parte*, if necessary.

(7) The Chief Commissioner or the Commissioner may on such terms as he deems fit and at any stage of the proceedings, adjourn the hearing of the complaint.

(8) The Chief Commissioner or the Commissioner shall decide the complaint as far as possible within a period of three months from the date of receipt of notice by the opposite party.

39. Advisory Committee to assist the Chief Commissioner. - (1) The Central Government shall appoint an Advisory Committee comprising of the following members, namely:-

(a) five experts to represent each of the five groups of specified disabilities mentioned in the Schedule to the Act of whom two shall be women;

(b) three experts in the field of barrier-free environment-

(i) one expert from physical environment;

(ii) one expert from transportation system; and

(iii) one expert from information and communication technology or other services and facilities provided to the public;

(c) one expert in the area of employment of persons with disabilities;

(d) one legal expert; and

(e) one expert as recommended by the Chief Commissioner for Persons with Disabilities.

(2) The Chief Commissioner may invite subject or domain expert as per the need who shall assist him in meeting or hearing and in preparation of the report.

(3) The tenure of the members of the Advisory Committee shall be for a period of three years and the members shall not be eligible for re-nomination.

(4) The non-official members of the Advisory Committee, in Delhi, shall be paid an allowance of rupees two thousand per day for each day of the actual meeting.

(5) The non-official members of the Advisory Committee, not residing in Delhi, shall be paid dailyallowance and travelling allowance for each day of the actual meeting at the rate admissible to a Group "A" officer of the Central Government.

40. Submission of Annual Report. - (1) The Chief Commissioner, shall as soon as possible, after the end of the financial year but not later than the 30th day of September in the next year ensuing prepare and submit to the Central Government, an annual report giving a complete account of his activities during the said financial year.

(2) In particular, the annual report referred to in sub-rule (1) shall contain information in respect of each of the following matters, namely:-

(a) names of its officers and staff and a chart showing the organisational set up;

(b) the functions which the Chief Commissioner has been empowered under sections 75 and 76 of the Act and the highlights of the performance in this regard;

(c) the main recommendations made by the Chief Commissioner;

(d) the progress made in the implementation of the Act; and

(e) any other matter deemed appropriate for inclusion by the Chief Commissioner or specified by the Central Government from time to time.

CHAPTER X

National Fund for Persons with Disabilities

41. Management of National Fund. - (1) There shall be a governing body consisting of following members to manage the National Fund, namely:-

(a) Secretary, Department of Empowerment of Persons with Disabilities, in the Central Government - Chairperson;

(b) Chairperson, Board of National Trust for the Welfare of Persons with Autism, Cerebral Palsy, Mental Retardation and Multiple Disabilities - Member;

(c) Financial Advisor, Ministry of Social Justice and Empowerment, in the Central Government - Member;

(d) two representatives from the Ministry of Health and Family Welfare, Department of School Education and Literacy, Department of Higher Education, Ministry of Labour and Employment, Department of Financial Services and Department of Rural Development in the Central Government, not below the rank of a Joint Secretary, by rotation in alphabetical order - Members;

(e) two persons representing different types of disabilities to be nominated by the Central Government, by rotation - Members;

(f) Joint Secretary in the Department of Empowerment of Persons with Disabilities in the Central Government - Convener and Chief Executive Officer.

(2) The governing body shall meet as often as necessary, but at least once in every financial year.

(3) The nominated members shall hold office for not more than three years.

(4) No member of the governing body shall be a beneficiary of the Fund during the period such member holds office.

(5) The nominated non-official members shall be eligible for payment of travelling allowance and daily allowance as admissible to a Group `A' employees of the Central Government for attending the meetings of the governing body.

(6) No person shall be nominated under clause (e) of sub-rule (1) as a member of the governing body if he -

(a) is, or has been, convicted of an offence, which in the opinion of the Central Government, involves moral turpitude; or

(b) is, or at any time has been, adjudicated as an insolvent.

42. Utilisation of the National Fund. - (1) The amount available under the Trust Fund for empowerment of persons with disabilities and the National Fund for people with disabilities, as on the date of the commencement of the Act, shall form the National Fund.

(2) All monies available under the two Funds referred to in sub-rule (1) shall stand transferred to the National Fund.

(3) All monies belonging to the Fund shall be deposited in such banks or invested in such manner as the governing body, may, subject to the general guidelines of the Central Government, decide.

(4) The Fund shall be invested in such manner as may be decided by the governing body.

(5) The Fund shall be utilized for the following purposes, namely:-

(a) financial assistance in the areas which are not specifically covered under any scheme and programme of the Central Government or are not adequately funded under any scheme or programme of the Central Government;

(b) for the purpose of implementation of the provisions of the Act;

(c) administrative and other expenses of the Fund, as may be required to be incurred by or under this Act; and

(d) such other purposes as may be decided by the governing body.

(6) Every proposal of expenditure shall be placed before the governing body for its approval.

(7) The governing body may appoint secretarial staff including accountants, with such terms and conditions, as it may think appropriate, to look after the management and utilisation of the Fund.

43. Budget. - The Chief Executive Officer of the Fund shall prepare the budget for incurring expenditure under the Fund for each financial year showing the estimated receipt and expenditure of the Fund, in January every year and shall place the same for consideration of the governing body.

44. Annual Report. - The annual report of the Department of Empowerment of Persons with Disabilities shall include a chapter on National Fund.

Legal rights of the disabled in India

- General legal provisions relating to the disabled lies in
- The disabled and the constitution
- Education Law for the Disabled
- Health Laws
- Family Laws
- Succession Laws for the Disabled
- Labour Laws for the Disabled
- Judicial procedures for the disabled
- Income Tax Concessions
- Relief for Handicapped
- The persons with disabilities (PWD) (equal opportunities, protection of rights and full participation) act, 1995
- Main Provisions of the Act
- Prevention and early detection of disabilities
- Education
- Employment
- Affirmative Action
- Non-Discrimination
- Research and Manpower Development
- Social Security
- Grievance Redressal
- The Mental Health Act, 1987

- The Rehabilitation Council of India Act, 1992
- The national trust for welfare of persons with autism, cerebral palsy, mental retardation and multiple disabilities act, 1999
- UN Declaration on the Rights of Mentally Retarded Persons

General legal provisions relating to the disabled lies in

1. Constitution
2. Education Laws
3. Health Laws
4. Family Laws
5. Succession laws
6. Labour Laws
7. Judicial Procedures
8. Income Tax Laws, &
9. Various Acts

- The Person with Disabilities Act, 1995
- The Mental Health Act, 1987
- The Rehabilitation Council of India, 1992
- The National Trust for Welfare of Persons with Autism, Cerebral Palsy, Mental Retardation, and Multiple Disabilities Act, 1999
- Declaration On The Rights Of Mentally Retarded Persons

The Disabled and the Constitution

The Constitution of India applies uniformly to every legal citizen of India, whether they are healthy or disabled in any way (physically or mentally)

Under the Constitution the disabled have been guaranteed the following fundamental rights:

1. The Constitution secures to the citizens including the disabled, a right of justice, liberty of thought, expression, belief, faith and worship, equality of status and of opportunity and for the promotion of fraternity.
2. Article 15(1) enjoins on the Government not to discriminate against any citizen of India (including disabled) on the ground of religion, race, caste, sex or place of birth.
3. Article 15 (2) States that no citizen (including the disabled) shall be subjected to any disability, liability, restriction or condition on any of the above grounds in the matter of their access to shops, public restaurants, hotels and places of public entertainment or in the use of wells, tanks, bathing ghats, roads and places of public resort maintained wholly or partly out of government funds or dedicated to the use of the general public. Women and children and those belonging to any socially and educationally backward classes or the Scheduled Castes & Tribes can be given the benefit of special laws or special provisions made by the State.
4. There shall be equality of opportunity for all citizens (including the disabled) in matters relating to employment or appointment to any office under the State.
5. No person including the disabled irrespective of his belonging can be treated as an untouchable. It would be an offence punishable in accordance with law as provided by Article 17 of the Constitution.

6. Every person including the disabled has his life and liberty guaranteed under Article 21 of the Constitution.
7. There can be no traffic in human beings (including the disabled), and beggar and other forms of forced labour is prohibited and the same is made punishable in accordance with law (Article 23).
8. Article 24 prohibits employment of children (including the disabled) below the age of 14 years to work in any factory or mine or to be engaged in any other hazardous employment. Even a private contractor acting for the Government cannot engage children below 14 years of age in such employment.
9. Article 25 guarantees to every citizen (including the disabled) the right to freedom of religion. Every disabled person (like the non-disabled) has the freedom of conscience to practice and propagate his religion subject to proper order, morality and health.
10. No disabled person can be compelled to pay any taxes for the promotion and maintenance of any particular religion or religious group.
11. No Disabled person will be deprived of the right to the language, script or culture which he has or to which he belongs.
12. Every disabled person can move the Supreme Court of India to enforce his fundamental rights and the rights to move the Supreme Court is itself guaranteed by Article 32.
13. No disabled person owning property (like the non-disabled) can be deprived of his property except by authority of law though right to property is not a fundamental right. Any unauthorized deprivation of

property can be challenged by suit and for relief by way of damages.

14. Every disabled person (like the non-disabled) on attainment of 18 years of age becomes eligible for inclusion of his name in the general electoral roll for the territorial constituency to which he belongs.

Education Law for the Disabled

- The right to education is available to all citizens including the disabled. Article 29(2) of the Constitution provides that no citizen shall be denied admission into any educational institution maintained by the State or receiving aid out of State funds on the ground of religion, race, caste or language.
- Article 45 of the Constitution directs the State to provide free and compulsory education for all children (including the disabled) until they attain the age of 14 years. No child can be denied admission into any educational institution maintained by the State or receiving aid out of State funds on the ground of religion, race, caste or language.

Health Laws

- Article 47 of the constitution imposes on the Government a primary duty to raise the level of nutrition and standard of living of its people and make improvements in public health - particularly to bring about prohibition of the consumption of intoxicating drinks and drugs which are injurious to one's health except for medicinal purposes.

- The health laws of India have many provisions for the disabled. Some of the Acts which make provision for the health of the citizens including the disabled may be seen in the Mental Health Act, 1987 (See later in the chapter).

Family Laws

Various laws relating to the marriage enacted by the Government for DIFFERENT communities apply equally to the disabled. In most of these Acts, it has been provided that the following circumstances will disable a person from undertaking a marriage. These are:

- Where either party is an idiot or lunatic,
- Where one party is unable to give valid consent due to unsoundness of mind or is suffering from a mental disorder of such a kind and extent as to be unfit for 'marriage for procreation of children'
- Where the parties are within the degree of prohibited relationship or are sapindas of each other unless permitted by custom or usage.
- Where either party has a living spouse

The rights and duties of the parties to the marriage, whether in respect of disabled or non-disabled persons are governed by the specific provisions contained in different marriage Acts, such as the Hindu Marriage Act, 1955, the Christian Marriage Act, 1872 and the Parsi Marriage and Divorce Act, 1935. Other marriage Acts that exist include; the Special Marriage Act, 1954 (for spouses of differing religions) and the Foreign Marriage Act, 1959 (for marriage outside India). The Child Marriage Restraint Act, 1929 as amended in 1978 to prevent the solemnization of child marriages also applies to the disabled. A Disabled person cannot act as a guardian of a minor under the Guardian and Wards Act, 1890 if the disability is of such a degree that one cannot act as a guardian of the minor. A similar position is taken by the Hindu Minority and Guardianship Act, 1956, as also under the Muslim Law

Succession Laws for the Disabled

Under the Hindu Succession Act, 1956 which applies to Hindus it has been provided explicitly that physical disability or physical deformity would not disentitle a person from inheriting ancestral property. Similarly, in the Indian Succession Act, 1925 which applies in the case of intestate and testamentary succession, there is no provision which deprives the disabled from inheriting ancestral property. The position with regard to Parsis and the Muslims is the same. In fact a disabled person can also dispose his property by writing a 'will' provided he understands the import and consequence of writing a will at the time when a will is written. For example, a person of unsound mind can make a Will during periods of sanity. Even blind persons or those who are deaf and dumb can make their Wills if they understand the import and consequence of doing it.

Labour Laws for the Disabled

The rights of the disabled have not been spelt out so well in the labour legislations but provisions which cater to the disabled in their relationship with the employer are contained in delegated legislations such as rules, regulations and standing orders.

Judicial procedures for the disabled

Under the Designs Act, 1911 which deals with the law relating to the protection of designs any person having jurisdiction in respect of the property of a disabled person (who is incapable of making any statement or doing anything required to be done under this Act) may be appointed by the Court under Section 74, to make such statement or do such thing in the name and on behalf of the person subject to the disability. The disability may be lunacy or other disability.

Income Tax Concessions

Relief for Handicapped

- **Section 80 DD:** Section 80 DD provides for a deduction in respect of the expenditure incurred by an individual or Hindu Undivided Family resident in India on the medical treatment (including nursing) training and rehabilitation etc. of handicapped dependants. For officiating the increased cost of such maintenance, the limit of the deduction has been raised from Rs.12000/- to Rs.20000/-.

- **Section 80 V:** A new section 80V has been introduced to ensure that the parent in whose hands income of a permanently disabled minor has been clubbed under Section 64, is allowed to claim a deduction upto Rs.20000/- in terms of Section 80 V.

- **Section 88B:** This section provides for an additional rebate from the net tax payable by a resident individual who has attained the age of 65 years. It has been amended to increase the rebate from 10% to 20%

in the cases where the gross total income does not exceed Rs.75000/- (as against a limit of Rs.50000/- specified earlier).

The persons with disabilities (PWD) (equal opportunities, protection of rights and full participation) act, 1995

"The Persons with Disabilities (Equal Opportunities, Protection of Rights and Full Participation) Act, 1995" had come into enforcement on February 7, 1996. It is a significant step which ensures equal opportunities for the people with disabilities and their full participation in the nation building. The Act provides for both the preventive and promotional aspects of rehabilitation like education, employment and vocational training, reservation, research and manpower development, creation of barrier- free environment, rehabilitation of persons with disability, unemployment allowance for the disabled, special insurance scheme for the disabled employees and establishment of homes for persons with severe disability etc.

Main Provisions of the Act

- Prevention and Early Detection of Disabilities
- Education
- Employment
- Non-Discrimination
- Research and Manpower Development
- Affirmative Action
- Social Security
- Grievance Redressal

Prevention and early detection of disabilities

- Surveys, investigations and research shall be conducted to ascertain the cause of occurrence of disabilities.
- Various measures shall be taken to prevent disabilities. Staff at the Primary Health Centre shall be trained to assist in this work.
- All the Children shall be screened once in a year for identifying 'at-risk' cases.
- Awareness campaigns shall be launched and sponsored to disseminate information.
- Measures shall be taken for pre-natal, peri natal, and post-natal care of the mother and child.

  Education
- Every Child with disability shall have the rights to free education till the age of 18 years in integrated schools or special schools.
- Appropriate transportation, removal of architectural barriers and restructuring of modifications in the examination system shall be ensured for the benefit of children with disabilities.
- Children with disabilities shall have the right to free books, scholarships, uniform and other learning material.
- Special Schools for children with disabilities shall be equipped with vocational training facilities.
- Non-formal education shall be promoted for children with disabilities.
- Teachers' Training Institutions shall be established to develop requisite manpower.

- Parents may move to an appropriate forum for the redressal of grievances regarding the placement of their children with disabilities.

Employment

3% of vacancies in government employment shall be reserved for people with disabilities, 1% each for the persons suffering from:

- Blindness or Low Vision
- Hearing Impairment
- Locomotor Disabilities & Cerebral Palsy
- Suitable Scheme shall be formulated for
- The training and welfare of persons with disabilities
- The relaxation of upper age limit
- Regulating the employment
- Health and Safety measures and creation of a non-handicapping, environment in places where persons with disabilities are employed

Government Educational Institutes and other Educational Institutes receiving grant from Government shall reserve at least 3% seats for people with disabilities.

No employee can be sacked or demoted if they become disabled during service,although they can be moved to another post with the same pay and condition. No promotion can be denied because of impairment.

Affirmative Action

Aids and Appliances shall be made available to the people with disabilities.

Allotment of land shall be made at concessional rates to the people with disabilities for:

- House
- Business
- Special Recreational Centres
- Special Schools
- Research Schools
- Factories by Entrepreneurs with Disability,

Non-Discrimination

- Public building, rail compartments, buses, ships and air-crafts will be designed to give easy access to the disabled people.
- In all public places and in waiting rooms, the toilets shall be wheel chair accessible. Braille and sound symbols are also to be provided in all elevators (lifts).
- All the places of public utility shall be made barrier-free by providing the ramps.

Research and Manpower Development

- Research in the following areas shall be sponsored and promoted
- Prevention of Disability
- Rehabilitation including community based rehabilitation
- Development of Assistive Devices.
- Job Identification
- On site Modifications of Offices and Factories
- Financial assistance shall be made available to the universities, other institutions of higher learning, professional bodies and non-government research- units

or institutions, for undertaking research for special education, rehabilitation and manpower development.

Social Security

- Financial assistance to non-government organizations for the rehabilitation of persons with disabilities.
- Insurance coverage for the benefit of the government employees with disabilities.
- Unemployment allowance to the people with disabilities who are registered with the special employment exchange for more than a year and could not find any gainful occupation

Grievance Redressal

- In case of violation of the rights as prescribed in this act, people with disabilities may move an application to the
- Chief Commissioner for Persons with Disabilities in the Centre, or
- Commissioner for Persons with Disabilities in the State.

The Mental Health Act, 1987

Under the Mental Health Act, 1987 mentally ill persons are entitled to the following rights:

1. A right to be admitted, treated and cared in a psychiatric hospital or psychiatric nursing home or convalescent home established or maintained by the Government or any other person for the treatment and care of mentally ill persons (other than the general hospitals or nursing homes of the Government).

2. Even mentally ill prisoners and minors have a right of treatment in psychiatric hospitals or psychiatric nursing homes of the Government.
3. Minors under the age of 16 years, persons addicted to alcohol or other drugs which lead to behavioral changes, and those convicted of any offence are entitled to admission, treatment and care in separate psychiatric hospitals or nursing homes established or maintained by the Government.
4. Mentally ill persons have the right to get regulated, directed and co-ordinated mental health services from the Government. The Central Authority and the State Authorities set up under the Act have the responsibility of such regulation and issue of licenses for establishing and maintaining psychiatric hospitals and nursing homes.
5. Treatment at Government hospitals and nursing homes mentioned above can be obtained either as in patient or on an out-patients basis.
6. Mentally ill persons can seek voluntary admission in such hospitals or nursing homes and minors can seek admission through their guardians. Admission can be sought for by the relatives of the mentally ill person on behalf of the latter. Applications can also be made to the local magistrate for grants of such (reception) orders.
7. The police have an obligation to take into protective custody a wandering or neglected mentally ill person, and inform his relative, and also have to produce such a person before the local magistrate for issue of reception orders.

8. Mentally ill persons have the right to be discharged when cured and entitled to 'leave' the mental health facility in accordance with the provisions in the Act.
9. Where mentally ill persons own properties including land which they cannot themselves manage, the district court upon application has to protect and secure the management of such properties by entrusting the same to a 'Court of Wards', by appointing guardians of such mentally ill persons or appointment of managers of such property.
10. The costs of maintenance of mentally ill persons detained as in-patient in any government psychiatric hospital or nursing home shall be borne by the state government concerned unless such costs have been agreed to be borne by the relative or other person on behalf of the mentally ill person and no provision for such maintenance has been made by order of the District Court. Such costs can also be borne out of the estate of the mentally ill person.
11. Mentally ill persons undergoing treatment shall not be subjected to any indignity (whether physical or mental) or cruelty. Mentally ill persons cannot be used without their own valid consent for purposes of research, though they could receive their diagnosis and treatment.
12. Mentally ill persons who are entitled to any pay, pension, gratuity or any other form of allowance from the government (such as government servants who become mentally ill during their tenure) cannot be denied of such payments. The person who is in-charge of such mentally person or his dependents will receive such payments after the magistrate has certified the same.

13. A mentally ill person shall be entitled to the services of a legal practitioner by order of the magistrate or district court if he has no means to engage a legal practitioner or his circumstances so warrant in respect of proceedings under the Act.

The Rehabilitation Council of India Act, 1992

This Act provides guarantees so as to ensure the good quality of services rendered by various rehabilitation personnel. Following is the list of such guarantees:

1. To have the right to be served by trained and qualified rehabilitation professionals whose names are borne on the Register maintained by the Council
2. To have the guarantee of maintenance of minimum standards of education required for recognition of rehabilitation qualification by universities or institutions in India.
3. To have the guarantee of maintenance of standards of professional conduct and ethics by rehabilitation professionals in order to protect against the penalty of disciplinary action and removal from the Register of the Council
4. To have the guarantee of regulation of the profession of rehabilitation professionals by a statutory council under the control of the central government and within the bounds prescribed by the statute

The national trust for welfare of persons with autism, cerebral palsy, mental retardation and multiple disabilities act, 1999

1. The Central Government has the obligation to set up, in accordance with this Act and for the purpose of the benefit of the disabled, the National Trust for Welfare of Persons with Autism, Cerebral Palsy, Mental Retardation and Multiple Disability at New Delhi.
2. The National Trust created by the Central Government has to ensure that the objects for which it has been set up as enshrined in Section 10 of this Act have to be fulfilled.
3. It is an obligation on part of the Board of Trustees of the National Trust so as to make arrangements for an adequate standard of living of any beneficiary named in any request received by it, and to provide financial assistance to the registered organizations for carrying out any approved programme for the benefit of disabled.
4. Disabled persons have the right to be placed under guardianship appointed by the 'Local Level Committees' in accordance with the provisions of the Act. The guardians so appointed will have the obligation to be responsible for the disabled person and their property and required to be accountable for the same.
5. A disabled person has the right to have his guardian removed under certain conditions. These include an abuse or neglect of the disabled, or neglect or misappropriation of the property under care.

6. Whenever the Board of Trustees are unable to perform or have persistently made default in their performance of duties, a registered organization for the disabled can complain to the central government to have the Board of Trustees superseded and/or reconstituted.
7. The National Trust shall be bound by the provisions of this Act regarding its accountability, monitoring finance, accounts and audit.

UN Declaration on the Rights of Mentally Retarded Persons

This declaration on the rights of mentally retarded person's calls for national and international actions so as to ensure that it will be used as a common basis and frame of reference for the protection of their rights:

1. The mentally retarded person has, to the maximum degree of feasibility, the same rights as under human beings.
2. The mentally retarded person has a right to proper medical care, physical therapy and to such education, training, rehabilitation and guidance which will enable him to further develop his ability, and reach maximum potential in life.
3. The mentally retarded person has a right of economic security and of a decent standard of living. He/she has a right to perform productive work or to participate in any other meaningful occupation to the fullest possible extent of capabilities.
4. Whenever possible, the mentally retarded person should live with his own family or with his foster parents and participate in different forms of community

life. The family with which he lives should receive assistance. If an institutional care becomes necessary then it should be provided in surroundings and circumstances as much closer as possible to that of a normal lifestyle.

5. The mentally retarded person has a right to a qualified guardian when this is required in order to protect his personal well-being or interests.
6. The mentally retarded person has a right to get protection from exploitation, abuse and a degrading treatment. If prosecuted for any offence; he shall have right to the due process of law, with full recognition being given to his degree of mental responsibility.
7. Whenever mentally retarded persons are unable (because of the severity of their handicap) to exercise their rights in a meaningful way or it should become necessary to restrict or deny some or all of their rights then the procedure(s) used for that restriction or denial of rights must contain proper legal safeguards against every form of abuse. This procedure for the mentally retarded must be based on an evaluation of their social capability by qualified experts, and must be subject to periodic review and a right of appeal to the higher authorities.

Source: ***A Handbook for Parents of Children with Disa***

https://drive.google.com/file/d/1-TDpRgunyJw22Q7758XU1xY-nr3inEP0/view

References

Agbenyega, JS., &Klibthong, S., (2014) Assessing Thai early childhood teachers'

agendas, International Journal of Inclusive Education, 22:10, 1048-1061, https://www.tandfonline.com/doi/full/10.1080/13603116.2017.1414578

Albalat, ST., Martínez, JRL., & García, OM. (2022). The inclusion of students who are most vulnerable to exclusion via cooperative learning. A longitudinal case-study. *European Journal of Special Needs Education,* https://www.tandfonline.com/doi/full/10.1080/08856257.2021.2021870

Amor, A.M., Hagiwara M., Shogren, KA., Thompson, JR., Verdugo, MA., Burke KM., & Aguayo, V. (2019). International perspectives and trends in research on inclusive education: A systematic review, *International Journal of Inclusive Education*, *23*(12), 1277-1295, https://www.tandfonline.com/doi/full/10.1080/13603116.2018.1445304

Annamma, A., Boelé, A., Moore, B., &Klingner, J. (2013). Challenging the ideology of normal in schools, *International Journal of Inclusive Education, 17*(12), 1278-1294,https://www.tandfonline.com/doi/full/10.1080/13603116.2013.802379

Antina, S. D., Johes, P., Luckner, J., Kreimeyer, K. H., & Reed, S. (2011). Social outcomes of students who are deaf and hard of hearing in general education classrooms. Exceptional Children, *77*(4), 489-504. https://journals.sagepub.com/doi/10.1177/001440291107700407

Attwood, S., MacArthur, J., & Kearney, A. (2019). Beginner secondary teacher preparedness for inclusion,*International Journal of Inclusive Education*, *23*(10), 1032-1048, https://www.tandfonline.com/doi/full/10.1080/13603116.2019.1625455

Baena, S., Sabé, JC., Molsosa, MG., & Manzano, M. (2022) More innovation, less inclusion? Debates and discussions regarding the intersectionality of innovation and inclusion in the Catalan school system: a position paper. *International Journal of Inclusive Education*, *26*(9), 865-877,https://www.tandfonline.com/doi/full/10.1080/13603116.2020.1736653

Baer, R. M., Daviso, A., Flexer, R. W., Queen, R. M., &Meindl, R. S. (2011). Students with intellectual disabilities: Predictors of transition outcomes. Career Development for Exceptional Individuals, *34*(3) 132-141.https://www.researchgate.net/publication/254081365_Students_With_Intellectual_Disabilities_Predictors_of_Transition_Outcomes

Bai, H., & Martin. S.M. (2015). Assessing the needs of training on inclusive education for public school administrators, *International Journal of Inclusive Education, 19*(12), 1229-1243.

https://www.tandfonline.com/doi/full/10.1080/13603116.2015.1041567

Bhatnagar, N. & Das, A. (2014). Attitudes of secondary school teachers towards inclusive education in New Delhi, India, *Journal of Research in Special Educational Needs, 14*(4), pp. 255-263. https://nasenjournals.onlinelibrary.wiley.com/doi/full/10.1111/14713802.12016

Brown, J.B. (2013). Including people with disabilities: An indigenous perspective,

InternationalJournal of Inclusive Education, 17(6), 571-583,https://www.tandfonline.com/doi/full/10.1080/13603116.2012.694483

Burçak A., B., Ballice, G., Bengisu, E., Korkmaz, S.A., &Paykoç, E., (2016) Embracing student experience in inclusive design education through learner-centred instruction, *International Journal of Inclusive Education, 20*(11), 1123-1141,https://www.tandfonline.com/doi/full/10.1080/13603116.2016.1155662

Chao, C.N.G., Chris Forlin, C., &Chuen, F. (2016). Improving teaching self-efficacy for teachers in inclusive classrooms in Hong Kong, *International Journal of Inclusive Education, 20*(11), 1142-1154.https://www.tandfonline.com/doi/ful l/10.1080/13603116.2016.1155663

Cheng, S., & Sin, F. (2018). Conceptions of learning and quality of university life among deaf, hard of hearing, and hearing university students, *International Journal of Inclusive Education, 22*(12), 1333-1344,

https://www.tandfonline.com/doi/full/10.1080/13603116.2018.1427154

Chin, M. (2020). The Zero Reject policy: a way forward for inclusive education in

Malaysia? *International Journal of Inclusive Education*, https://www.tandfonline.com/doi/full/10.1080/13603116.2020.1846800

Corcoran, T., Claiborne, L., & Whitburn. (2019). Paradoxes in inclusive education: a

necessary condition of relationality? *International Journal of Inclusive Education, 23*(10), 1003-1016, https://www.tandfonline.com/doi/full/10.1080/13603116.2019.1625453

Damianidou, E. (2021). Curriculum and the power to ex(in)clude disabled students, *International Journal of Inclusive Education*, https://www.tandfonline.com/doi/full/10.1080/13603116.2021.1994034

Damianidou, E. &Phtiaka, H. (2018) Implementing inclusion in disabling settings: the role of teachers' attitudes and practices, *International Journal of Inclusive Education, 22*(10), 1078-1092,https://www.tandfonline.com/doi/full/10.1080/13603116.2017.1415381

Dare, L., & Nowicki, E. (2020). 'The road less travelled': Grade-level acceleration in

Inclusive schools, *International Journal of Inclusive Education*, https://www.tandfonline.com/doi/full/10.1080/13603116.2020.1837265

Das, A. K., Kuyini A. B., & Desai I. P. (2013). Inclusive education in India: are the teachers prepared? *International Journal of Special Education.28*(1). http://www.internationaljournalofspecialeducation.com/articles.cfm?y=2013&v=28&n=1

Davies, M., Elliott, S.N., & Cumming, J. (2016). Documenting support needs and adjustment gaps for students with disabilities: teacher practices in Australian classrooms and on national tests, *International Journal of Inclusive Education, 20*(12), 1252-1269, https://www.tandfonline.com/doi/full/10.1080/13603116.2016.1159256

Delorey, J., Specht, J., Fairbrother, M., Ismailos, L., Villella, M., Charles, E., Vanderloon, M., Gallagher, T., Howell, G., & Whitley, J. (2020). Experiences that shape pre-service teachers' inclusive practice beliefs: a group concept mapping study, *International Journal of Inclusive Education.* https://www.tandfonline.com/doi/full/10.1080/13603116.2020.1862403

Devi, U. & Reddy, A. (2016). Problems of children with special needs (CWSNS) in

accessing the education: Role of barrier free environment – A case study of India. *Bulgarian Journal of Science and Education Policy,10*(1). http://bjsep.org/getfile .php?id=209

Dewilde, J., &Skrefsrud, T. (2016). Including alternative stories in the mainstream. How transcultural young people in Norway perform creative cultural resistance in and outside of school. *International Journal of Inclusive Education, 20*(10), 1032-1042.

https://www.tandfonline.com/doi/full/10.1080/13603116.2016.1145263

Dodd, E., Ellis, S., &Sonal, S. (2020). Making the invisible, visible: a twenty-first century approach to tertiary preparation, attainment and access for student equity, *International Journal of Inclusive Education*,https://www.tandfonline.com/doi/full/10.1080/13603116.2020.1831629

Fandrem, H. Jahnsen, H. Nergaard, S. &Tveitereid, K. (2021). Inclusion of immigrant

students in schools: the role of introductory classes and other segregatedefforts, *International Journal of Inclusive Education,* https://www.tandfonline.com/doi/full/10.1080/13603116.2021.1950222

Fırat, T., Bildiren, A., &Demiral, N. (2021). The change in reactions of preschool children to physical disability: a parent-Supported intervention, *European Journal of Special Needs Education*, https://www.tandfonline.com/doi/full/10.1080/08856257.2021.2013548

Freixenet, J., Vantieghem, W., Gheyssens, E., &Struyven, K. (2020). Connecting beliefs, noticing, and differentiated teaching practices: a study among pre-service teachers and teachers, *International Journal of Inclusive Education*,https://www.tandfonline.com/doi/full/10.1080/13603116.2020.1862404

Garwood, J., & Christopher, L., Loan, V. (2019). Pre-service educators' dispositions toward inclusive practices for students with emotional and behavioural difficulties, *International Journal of Inclusive Education*, *23*(12), 1332-

1347, https://www.tandfonline.com/doi/full/10.1080/13603116.2018.1447614

Ginevra, M., Maggio, I., Valbusa, I., Santilli, S., & Nota, L. (2021). Teachers' attitudes

towards students with disabilities: the role of the type of information provided in the students' profiles of children with disabilities, *European Journal of Special Needs Education*, https://www.tandfonline.com/doi/full/10.1080/08856257.2021.1878658

Government of India. National Policy on Education, 1986 (As modified in 1992). National Policy on Education, 1986 (As modified in 1992)https://www.education.gov.in/en/national-policy-education-1986-modified-1992

Graham, L.J. (2018). Student compliance will not mean 'all teachers can teach': a critical analysis of the rationale for 'no excuses' discipline. International Journal of Inclusive Education, *22*(11), 1242-1256, https://www.tandfonline.com/doi/full/10.1080/13603116.2017.1420254

Gubbels, J., Coppens, K., & Wolf, I. (2018). Inclusive education in the Netherlands: how funding arrangements and demographic trends relate to dropout and participation rates, *International Journal of Inclusive Education, 22*(11), 1137 - 1153,https://www.tandfonline.com/doi/full/10.1080/13603116.2017.1416684

Hamilton, C., &Kecskemeti, M. (2015) Beginning teachers reflect on inclusive practices – 'I didn't realize that he only had half a hand', *International Journal of Inclusive Education, 19*(12), 1265-1279, https://www.tandfonline.com/doi/full/10.1080/13603116.2015.1055341

Hanssen, N., &Erina, I. (2021). Parents' views on inclusive education for children with special educational needs in Russia, *European Journal of Special Needs Education*,https://www.tandfonline.com/doi/full/10.1080/08856257.2021.1949092

Harrison, J., Denise, A., Soares & Joyce, J. (2019). Inclusion of students with emotional and behavioural disorders in general education settings: a scoping review of research in the US, *International Journal of Inclusive Education, 23*(12), 1209-1231,https://www.tandfonline.com/doi/full/10.1080/13603116.2018.1444107

Hassan U.M. (2015) Attitudes of school heads towards inclusion of student with disabilities in regular schools, *Journal of Educational Sciences & Research, 2*(1), pp 59-70.https://www.researchgate.net/publication/330170338_Attitudes_of_School _Headstowards_Inclusion_of_Student_with_Disabilities_in _Regular_Schools

Helmer, J., Kasa, R., Somerton, M., Michael, T., &Torrano, D. (2020). Planting the seeds for inclusive education: one resource centre at a time, *International Journal of InclusiveEducation,* https://www.tandfonline.com/doi/full/10.1080/13603116.20 20.1864791

Heng, L., Quinlivan, K., & Plessis, R. (2019). Exploring the creation of a new initial teacher education (ITE)

programme underpinned by inclusion, *International Journal of Inclusive Education, 23*(10), 1017-1031, https://cogentoa.tandfonline.com/doi/full/10.1080/13603116.2019.1625454

Iacono, T., Landry, O., Melgar, A., Jo Spong, Hyett, N., Bagley K., & McKinstry, C. (2021). A systematized review of co-teaching efficacy in enhancing inclusive education for students with disability, *International Journal of Inclusive Education*,https://www.tandfonline.com/doi/full/10.1080/13603116 .2021.1900423

Jha, M. M. (2010) From Special To Inclusive Education In India: Case Studies Of Three Schools In Delhi. https://www.google.co.in/books/edition/From_Special_To_Inclusive_Education_In_I/JxiZjWgDwlYC?hl=en&gbpv=1&dq=case+study+on+special+school+in+india&pg=PP10&printsec=frontcover

Johansson, S. (2014). A critical and contextual approach to inclusive education: perspectives from an Indian context. *International Journal of Inclusive Education*, *18*(12), 1219-1236, http://dx.doi.org/10.1080/08856257.2022.2031096

Julia M. White, Meghan Cosier&Qiu Wang. (2023). Exploring factors related to access to general education contexts for students with intellectual disability: a survey of district special education administrators in one state, International Journal of Inclusive Education, 27(1), 35-53. https://www.tandfonline.com/doi/full/10.1080/13603116.2020.1818140

Kelly, N. (2014). Does equal access mean treat the same? From theory to practice in the classroom of English as an

Additional Language learner in Ireland – towards a transformative agenda.*International Journal of Inclusive Education, 18*(9), 857-876, https://www.tandfonline.com/doi/full/10.1080/13603116.2013.855264

Kern., A. (2020). Who is in and who is out: parents' views on barriers to learning, *International Journal of Inclusive Education*, https://www.tandfonline.com/doi/full/10.1080/13603116.2020.1853254

Kilinc, S. (2019). 'Who will fit in with whom?' Inclusive education struggles for students with disabilities, *International Journal of Inclusive Education, 23*(12), 1296-1314, https://www.tandfonline.com/doi/full/10.1080/13603116.2018.1447612

Korsgaard, M., & Mortensen, S. (2017). Towards a shift in perspective for inclusive education research – a continental approach, *International Journal of Inclusive Education, 21*(12), 1245-1260,https://www.tandfonline.com/doi/full/10.1080/13603116.2017.1335356

Larsen, T., Holloway, J., & Hamre, B. (2019). How is an inclusive agenda possible in an excluding education system? Revisiting the Danish Dilemma, *International Journal of Inclusive Education, 23*(10), 1049-1064,https://www.tandfonline.com/doi/full/10.1080/13603116.2019.1626497

Lie, J.H. (2022). Student participation in dialogue in individual subject curriculum meetings: students' and parents' perceptions. *International Journal of Inclusive*

Education, 26(9), 913-926,https://www.tandfonline.com/doi/full/10.1080/13603116.2020.1749945

Lohmann, A., Wulfekühler, H., Wiedebusch, S., &Hensen, G. (2019). Parents' attitudes towards inclusive education in day care facilities, *International Journal of Inclusive Education, 23*(12), 1232-1247, https://www.tandfonline.com/doi/full/10.1080/13603116.2018.1444106

Main, S., Chambers, D., & Sarah, P. (2016). Supporting the transition to inclusive education: teachers' attitudes to inclusion in the Seychelles, *International Journal of Inclusive Education, 20*(12), 1270-1285,https://www.tandfonline.com/doi/full/10.1080/13603116.2016.1168873

McAnelly, K., & Gaffney, K. (2019). Rights, inclusion and citizenship: a good news story about learning in the early years, *International Journal of Inclusive Education, 23*(10), 1081-1094,https://www.tandfonline.com/doi/full/10.1080/13603116.2019.1629123

Meadows, ML. & Caniglia, J. (2018). Co-teacher noticing: implications for professional development, *International Journal of Inclusive Education,* 22(12), 1345-1362https://www.tandfonline.com/doi/full/10.1080/13603116. 2017.1420827

Mintz, J., & Wyse, D. (2015). Inclusive pedagogy and knowledge in special education: addressing the tension, *International Journal of Inclusive Education, 19*(11), 1161-1171,

https://www.tandfonline.com/doi/full/10.1080/13603116.2015.1044203

Molbaek, M. (2018). Inclusive teaching strategies – dimensions and agendas, *International Journal of Inclusive Education, 22*(10), 1048-1061,https://www.tandfonline.com/doi/full/10.1080/13603116.2017.1414578

Mortier, K., Hunt, P., Leroy, M., Putte, I.V.d., & Hove, G.V. (2010). Communities of practice in inclusive education, *Educational Studies, 36*(3), 345-355,https://www.tandfonline.com/doi/full/10.1080/03055690903424816

NCERT (2006). Including Children and Youth with disabilities in Education, a Guide for Practitioners. Department of Education of Groups with Special Needs. New Delhi: National Council of Educational Research and Training. Available on http://ncert.nic.in

NCERT (1998). Sixth All-India educational survey. New Delhi: National Council of Educational Research and Training. Right to Persons with Special Needs Act 2016. https://legislative.gov.in/sites/default/files/A2016-49_1.pdf

Nusbaum, E. (2013). Vulnerable to exclusion: the place for segregated education within conceptions of inclusion, *International Journal of Inclusive Education, 17*(12), 1295-1311. https://www.tandfonline.com/doi/full/10.1080/13603116.2013.826292

Nuth, M. (2018). Learning from experience: towards inclusive educational research in

Cambodia, International Journal of Inclusive Education, 22:11, 1184-1196,https://www.tandfonline.com/doi/full/10.1080/13603116.2017.1418440

Nyborg, G., Mjelve, L., Edwards, A., & Crozier, W. (2022). Teachers' strategies for enhancing shy children's engagement in oral activities: necessary, but insufficient? *International Journal of Inclusive Education*, *26*(7), 643-658.

Orlando, A.M., Klinepeter, E., & Foster, M. (2016). Retrospectives on factors influencing inclusive opportunities for college students with extensive support needs, *International Journal of Inclusive Education, 20*(12), 1239-1251, https://www.tandfonline.com/doi/full/10.1080/13603116.2016.1159255

Pastore, G. (2018). Inclusion and social exclusion issues in university education in prison: considerations based on the Italian and Spanish experiences, *International Journal of Inclusive Education, 22*(12), 1272-1287,https://www.tandfonline.com/doi/full/10.1080/13603116.2018.1426050

Paulsrud D., &Nilholm, C. (2020). Teaching for inclusion – a review of research on the cooperation between regular teachers and special educators in the work with students in need of special support, *International Journal of Inclusive Education*, https://www.tandfonline.com/doi/full/10.1080/13603116.2020.184 6799

Ralls, D. (2019). 'Becoming co-operative' – challenges and insights: repositioning school engagement as a collective endeavour, *International Journal of Inclusive Education, 23*(11), 1134-1148, https://www.tandfonline.com/doi/ful l/10.1080/13 603116.2019.1629159

Rich, B. (2020). How are culturally inclusive teaching practices integrated into business school's curriculum? An analysis of syllabi from the United States, *International Journal of Inclusive Education,*https://www.tandfonline.com/doi/full/10.1080/ 13603116.2020.1846798

Rosea, R. (2017) Seeking practice informed policy for inclusive education in India. *AJIE Asian Journal of Inclusive Education*, Vol. 5. No. 1, July 2017, *5*(22).

Russak, S. (2016). Do inclusion practices for pupils with special educational needs in the English as a foreign language class in Israel reflect inclusion laws and language policy requirements? *International Journal of Inclusive Education,* *20*(11), 11881203, https://www.tandfonline.com/doi/full/10 .1080/13603116.2016.1155666

Satherley D., & Norwich, B. (2021). Parents' experiences of choosing a special school for their children, *European Journal of Special Needs Education*, https://www.tandf online.com/doi/full/10.1080/08856257.2021.1967298

Schneider, C. (2015). Social participation of children and youth with disabilities in Canada, France and Germany, *International Journal of Inclusive Education, 19(10),* 1068-

1079,https://www.tandfonline.com/doi/full/10.1080/136031 16.2015 .1037867

Scholes, L., Brownlee, J., Walker, S., & Johansson, E. (2017). Changes in children's reasoning about the social inclusion of aggressive children over the early years of elementary school, *International Journal of Inclusive Education, 21*(10)991-1010. https://www.tandfonline.com/doi/full/10.1080/13603116.20 17.132 5075

Schostak. J., (2019) 'Towards a society of equals': democracy, education, cooperation and the practice of radical inclusion, *International Journal of Inclusive Education, 23*(11), 1103-1115, https://www.tandfonline.com/doi/full/10.1080/136 03116.2019.1629161

Schurig, M., Weib, S., Kiel, E., Heimlich, U., & Gebhardt, M. (2020). Assessment of the quality of inclusive schools A short form of the quality scale of inclusive school development (QU!S-S) – reliability, factorial structure and measurement invariance, *International Journal of Inclusive Education,*https://www.tandfonline. com/doi/full/10.1080/13603116.2020.1862405

Schwab, S., Resch K., &Alnahdi, G. (2021). Inclusion does not solely apply to students with disabilities: pre-service teachers' attitudes towards inclusive schooling of all students, *International Journal of Inclusive Education,*https://www.tandfo nline.com/doi/full/10.1080/13603116.2021.1938712

Sherfinski, M., Weekley, B.S., & Mathew, S. (2015). Reconceptualising advocacy: creating inclusive education in US universal pre-kindergarten, *International Journal of Inclusive Education, 19*(12), 1213-1228,https://www.tandfonline.com/doi/full/10.1080/13603116.2015.1041566

Sigstad, HMH., Holmberg &Morken, I. (2021). Succeeding in inclusive practices in school in Norway – A qualitative study from a teacher perspective, European Journal of Special Needs Education. https://www.tandfonline.com/doi/full/10.1080/08856257.2021.1997481

Singal, N. (2006). An ecosystemic approach for understanding inclusive education: An Indian case study. European Journal of Psychology of Education, 21. https://doi.org/10.1007/BF03173413

Singal, N. (2005). Mapping the field of inclusive education: A review of the Indian

literature. *International Journal of Inclusive Education* 9(4), 331-350 https://www.tandfonline.com/doi/full/10.1080/13603110500138277

Sirem, O. &Çatal, T. (2022). An analysis of classroom teachers' awareness of inclusive education, *European Journal of Special Needs Education,* https://www.tandfonline.com/doi/full/10.1080/08856257.2022.2050971

Slee, R. (2019). Belonging in an age of exclusion, *International Journal of Inclusive Education, 23*(9), 909-922, https://www.tandfonline.com/doi/full/10.1080/13603116.2019.1602366

Strogilos, V. (2012). The cultural understanding of inclusion and its development within a centralised system, *International Journal of Inclusive Education, 16*(12), 1241-1258,https://www.tandfonline.com/doi/full/10.1080/13603116. 2011.557447

Subban, P., Bradford, B., Sharma, U., Loreman, T., Avramidis, E., Kullmann, H., Lozano, C., Romano, A., & Woodcock, S., (2022) Does it really take a village to raise a child? Reflections on the need for collective responsibility in inclusive education, *European Journal of Special Needs Education*, https://www.tandfonline.com/doi/full/10.1080/08856257.2022.2059632

Symeonidou, S. (2022). Teacher education for inclusion and anti-oppressive curriculum development: innovative approaches informed by disability arts and narratives, *International Journal of Inclusive Education, 26*(7), 659-673,https://www.tandfonline.com/doi/full/10.1080/13603116.2020.1711819

Tan, R., Lichtblau, M., Wehmeier, C., &Werning, R. (2021). Preschool teachers' attitudes towards inclusion: A comparison study between China and Germany, *European Journal of Special Needs Education*,https://www.tandfonline.com/doi/full/10.1080/08856257.2021.1997480

Tawanda Majoko, T. (2017). Inclusion in early childhood education: a Zimbabwean perspective, *International Journal of Inclusive Education, 21*(12), 1210-1227,https://www.tandfonline.com/doi/full/10.1080/13603116.2017.1335354

The Rehabilitation Council of India Act (1992).https://legislative.gov.in/actsofparliamentfromtheyear/rehabilitation-council-india-act-1992

Timberlake, M.T. (2017). Nice, but we can't afford it: challenging austerity and finding abundance in inclusive education, *International Journal of Inclusive Education, 22*(9), 954-968,https://www.tandfonline.com/doi/full/10.1080/13603116.2017.1412518

Torrano, DH., Somerton, M., & Helmer, J. (2022). Mapping research on inclusive education since Salamanca Statement: a bibliometric review of the literature over 25 years, International Journal of Inclusive Education, 26:9, 893-912,https://www.tandfonline.com/doi/full/10.1080/13603116.2020.1747555

Tracey, D., Barker, K., Valuka, P., Baambu, W., Gene, K., Moko, E., Robert, S., Robin, G., Sowi, C., Wanis, J., Wine, D., Nelson, G., &Arifeae, P. (2021). Furthering inclusive education in Papua New Guinea through teacher training: reflections on challenges and transformations, *International Journal of Inclusive Education*,https://www.tandfonline.com/doi/full/10.1080/13603116.2021.1941321

UNICEF (2012). The right of children with disabilities to education: A rights-based approach to Inclusive Education. *Position Paper.https://www.unicef.org/media/126506/file/UNICEF-Right-to-Education-Children-Disabilities ENG.pdf*

Vallee, D. (2017). Student engagement and inclusive education: reframing student engagement, *International Journal of Inclusive Education, 21*(9), 920-937, https://www.tandfonline.com/doi/full/10.1080/13603116.2017.1296033

Wilkins, C. (2015). Education reform in England: quality and equity in the performative school, *International Journal of Inclusive Education, 19*(11), 1143-1160,https://www.tandfonline.com/doi/full/10.1080/13603116.2015.10 44202

Ytterhus, B., &Åmot, I. (2021). Kindergartens: inclusive spaces for all children? *International Journal of Inclusive Education.* https://cogentoa.tandf online.com/doi/full/10.1080/13603116.2021.1950976

Zano, K. (2020). From the teachers' perspectives: resources used in teaching reading comprehension to English First Additional Language (EFAL) learners in the FET phase, *International Journal of Inclusive Education*,https://www.tandfonline.com /doi/full/10.1080/13603116.2020.1858979